Youth Ministry and Wilderness Camping

ERIK C. MADSEN

D0768084

Judson Press ® Valley Forge

YOUTH MINISTRY AND WILDERNESS CAMPING

Copyright © 1982
Judson Press, Valley Forge, PA 19481

Unless otherwise indicated, the Scripture quotations in this publication are from the Revised Standard Version of the Bible copyrighted 1946, 1952 © 1971, 1973 by the Division of Christian Education of the National Council of the Churches of Christ in the U.S.A., and used by permission.

Other versions of the Bible quoted in this book are:

The Jerusalem Bible, copyright © 1966 by Darton, Longman & Todd, Ltd. and Doubleday and Company, Inc. Used by permission of the publisher.

The Living Bible, Tyndale House Publishers, Wheaton, Ill. Used by permission.

The New English Bible, Copyright © The Delegates of the Oxford University Press and The Syndics of the Cambridge University Press, 1961, 1970.

Library of Congress Cataloging in Publication Data

Madsen, Erik C.
  Youth ministry and wilderness camping.

  Bibliography: p.
  Includes index.
  1. Christian education, Outdoor. 2. Christian education of young people. 3. Wilderness survival.
I. Title.
BV1587.M33   268'.6   82-15269
ISBN 0-8170-0962-0   AACR2

The name JUDSON PRESS is registered as a trademark in the U.S. Patent Office.
Printed in the U.S.A. ✛

TO

THE

MEMBERS

AND FRIENDS

OF QUEEN ANNE

BAPTIST CHURCH,

SEATTLE, WASHINGTON,

WHOSE LOVING ENCOURAGEMENT

OF MY INVOLVEMENT WITH YOUTH

IN WILDERNESS CAMPING MINISTRIES

HAS

MADE

THIS

BOOK POSSIBLE

Contents

Preface 7

Introduction: The Challenge of Wilderness Christian Education   9

Part I The Value of Wilderness Christian Education   17

    Chapter 1 Wilderness Experiential Education:

           A Christian Perspective **19**

    Chapter 2 Understanding Adolescence: Guidelines for

           Involvement in Wilderness Education .   **43**

    Chapter 3 The Wilderness Ethos and Christian

           Education: A Biblical Perspective **57**

Part II The Practice of Wilderness Christian Education **73**

    Chapter 4 The Wilderness Leader **75**

    Chapter 5 Special Skills for Wilderness Learning **91**

    Chapter 6 The Wilderness Experience **107**

Conclusion: Wilderness Experiential Education: Affirmative

        Values **123**

Appendix A Devotional Guides **127**

Appendix B Equipment List **137**

Appendix C Sample Letters **139**

Appendix D Special Concerns **141**

Appendix E Sample Menu **143**

Appendix F Fitness Helps **145**

Notes **147**

Resource Bibliography **153**

Index **157**

Preface

I had my first serious exposure to the rigors of extended wilderness trail camping during the summer of 1969. In August of that year my eldest son and I set out to undertake what in our minds would be a monumental achievement. We would hike across the Washington Cascades from west to east. We would take approximately a week to accomplish this, carrying all the ingredients for our survival on our backs.

I know now that there were informational resources available, just waiting to be utilized by the would-be backcountry traveler, but I wasn't sure where to look or with whom to make contact. Hearsay, plus a smattering of common sense, became our guide. We did our best, discovering the hard way that there are better ways to go than with eight-pound sleeping bags, an ultraheavy canvas pup tent, fishing waders, and some instant foods that even our dog refused to eat!

We staggered into the wilderness with sixty-five-pound packs, really excited about this adventure. What happened during that week was the beginning of an intense love affair with the pristine environment of a wilderness area dominated by Glacier Peak in the North Cascades of Washington. The psalmist had warned me that God had prepared some breathtaking beauty for God's creatures to enjoy—but I had completely underestimated what that beauty might be!

We survived. Indeed, we did surprisingly well! And the insights which came during that forty-mile trek gave birth to an intense desire to use the opportunities provided in wilderness trail camping to meet the religious, educational, social, and physical needs of our church youth. I determined to invest a portion of each summer in researching and developing a more adequate ministry to youth along these lines.

This manual has grown out of the experience of more than a decade. I have discovered, contrary to the bleak headlines we too often read, that we are blessed with many quality young people in our land. Many are looking to the church for guidance. They are genuinely interested in discovering God's purpose for their lives. Living with young people in a wilderness setting, removed from the cultural paraphernalia on which we depend too much, I found that we learned quickly to appreciate the resources within and around us. Such learning can be used effectively in achieving the objectives of Christian education.

I have attempted, through this manual, to put at our fingertips a majority of the resources which I have found to be helpful in the planning and programming of trail camping. I am concerned that we make the most of a God-given opportunity to challenge and win young people to a deeper experience of the Christian faith, as well as nurture them in a productive relationship to the kingdom of God.

I am indebted to many persons, counselors and youth alike, who have shared wilderness trail camps with me. They have been most helpful as I have struggled to discover the intricacies of the planning, preparation, and execution that make a church-oriented trail experience successful. Because of their patience, helpful insights, and encouragement in getting this material together, this manual has become a reality.

I am deeply grateful for the wise counsel and perceptive critiquing offered to me by Dr. Harold Frazee, now retired from the American Baptist Seminary of the West. His insights from a lifetime of teaching as well as his great interest in wilderness camping have been invaluable. Gaylord Hasseblad, our Region Minister of Camping, was most helpful to me with his scholarly assessment of grammar and style, forcing me to express myself more clearly in all areas of this undertaking. Harry Swetnam, fitness expert extraordinaire, has been my mentor in keeping my body physically fit and has offered much appreciated counsel on the values of various techniques of physical fitness in preparation for wilderness hiking. The prime mover in bringing this manual to completion has been my wife, who labored for hour after hour through page after page of typing and who—when the frustrations of writing made me most unlovable—still loved me!

If this manual assists even one trail camp director or one counselor to enable a young person to call forth inner resources and to appropriate God's power to help him or her to become a more mature person in Christ through the rigors of the wilderness experience, all our efforts will have been rewarded.

Introduction: The Challenge of Wilderness Christian Education

A serious look at the ministry of the church to today's youth reveals a variety of styles which have varying degrees of effectiveness. Many forms of ministry are committed to a traditional approach to Christian education, patterned after the conventional model of secular classroom education. The physical setting varies only as much as creative use of chairs, desks, walls, and other classroom accessories will permit. Creativity can provide interesting variations to the instructional format, but basically the intention is to present the student with data considered important to shape that student into a knowledgeable and productive participant in society. Creative new programs have made a great number of imaginative, important, and relevant contributions to the church's ministry to youth, with observable influences on the lives of young people. At the heart of this creativity is the awareness that

> it is not wise to depend on our own short, unreflective pasts or on our current endeavors to provide insight for the future, for when we do, we too easily accept the established as real. *The future is in our imaginations and with God.* In that conviction is our hope[1] (author's italics).

I am not suggesting that we abandon the traditional approach. I hope we will continue to explore the possibilities of improving methods that, in many instances, have served the church well. But, along with this, I am most hopeful that new ministries will be researched and developed which will provide additional opportunities to meet the theological and educational needs of our youth. We must exercise our imaginations and trust God to stimulate us to new expressions of creativity in ministry.

The church schools with which I am familiar have contact with their students for an average of one hour weekly, or fifty-two hours annually.

More and more church schools are suspending activities during the summer months, resulting in an even smaller number of hours annually for student contact. I believe many teachers will agree that, given the weekly or annual time limitation, the ministry of the church school to our youth is severely inadequate.

One new form of ministry that is becoming increasingly popular is wilderness trail camping. This is a ministry that has developed out of the church's interest in camping as a respectable addition to the methods of providing Christian education for its youth. It is a ministry with great potential. Will it ever be brought to maturity as an accepted extension of the church's Christian educational ministry?

The church's educational ministry has the goal of helping a person toward becoming a whole person in a redemptive context. We are not yet what we have the potential of becoming in Jesus Christ. Because we have chosen to reject, or ignore, the divine pattern for our lives, we are included in the statement that "*all* have sinned and fall short of the glory of God" (Romans 3:23). Our only alternative is re-creation, "If any one is in Christ, he is a *new creation* (2 Corinthians 5:17) (author's italics). The epitome of being, according to Jesus Christ, is to love God "with all your heart, and with all your soul, and with all your mind" and to "love your neighbor as yourself" (Matthew 22:37, 39). This is possible only as we move toward wholeness through re-creation.

Christian education, in its variety of forms, helps us to move toward that goal. I say *move* because there is no static wholeness; the process is continuous. Christian education should have, as one of its aims, the involvement of youth and adults in experiences in which the Spirit of God will find freedom to work at encouraging the individual toward becoming a whole person in Christ. Our goal is not the manipulation of personality. It is rather to seek for and develop situations, conditions, and opportunities through which the grace of God can become redemptive.

The framework in which this process takes place is described as follows:

> Every self has a past which determines to a considerable extent what the present shall be. Also, every self has its future; that is, the possibilities which are relevant to it. The self, with its past flowing into it and with the possibilities for the next moment converging upon it, must come to some determination as to what it will become in this instant of the passage of time.[2]

God, working in and through this framework, can encourage the self to react intentionally, thus becoming the new creation God intends. In the process of becoming, the new person in Christ discovers what it means to relate, in love, to self, others, and all of God's creation. "We are to grow up in every way into him who is the head, into Christ, from whom the whole body, joined and knit together by every joint with which it is supplied, when each part is working properly, makes bodily growth and upbuilds itself in love" (Ephesians 4:15-16). Christian education is concerned with the ongoing flow of this process—each individual rising to full potential in Jesus Christ. This occurs most effectively in the community of faith.

Wilderness Christian education affords a unique and creative opportunity to grow in Christ within a community of faith. It is quite possible that this might be experienced at a depth of involvement not usually encountered in the traditional Christian education process. When our response to God is made with keen sensitivity to our involvement in the experiential *now,* past realities come alive in the present moment. Role playing, an effective tool in the classroom, does not have the impact of an actual field experience! The wilderness traveler, carrying a double pack to assist an injured trailmate, experiences a teachable moment on the concept of Christ's suffering for us. The message of God's love is reflected in the present reality of caring hands ministering to a youth's blistered feet! Once an experience has been lived through, however, role playing may be used to recapture the essence of that experience in a later teaching session.

There is no uniform process. To attempt to deal with young people in a production-line manner is to ignore the uniqueness of each emerging individual self. The leader's awareness of youth in the process of becoming mature persons encompasses all phases of development including the awareness of their physical, social, psychological, and religious characteristics and needs.

I see the Bible as an important resource calling us to a realization of what we might become. However, if the manner in which the Bible is presented is designed to do our thinking for us, its use will be ineffective. The message of the Bible probes at our reasons for "doing." It should never be used in such a way that it separates "thinking" from "doing." God confronts us in the Bible; we should never minimize this fact. That confrontation generates a free response from us: an intelligent, thoughtful response of our total self to the self-disclosure of God. In addition to this confrontation through reported experiences, God also confronts us through the lives of those who live out the biblical message.

Wilderness Christian education has the exciting potential for encouraging a community of love in which each participant may discover faith, hope, love, and selfhood in new ways. If those in the leadership roles are deeply involved in the process of becoming new persons, those with whom they minister may find God revealed afresh in a warm, spontaneous, caring fellowship. Leaders involved in the struggle to become new persons should be aware of their own vulnerability. When a counselor becomes super-tired, experiences body aches and pains from a difficult day on the trail, is wretched in spirit, and yet is able to grapple with all these feelings—mental, physical, spiritual—the discovery of faith, hope, love, and selfhood can take place in new ways within the supportive fellowship of the group.

Youth are perceptive. They see the process of becoming at work. This frees them to exercise their personal faith, hope, love, and selfhood, and find the redemptive power of the biblical message coming alive in a human life. Youth will be more able to place their trust in a God whom they have not seen when they are able to have basic trust in a human being they have seen. The responsibility is awesome but rewarding.

As we consider the development, and legitimizing of the wilderness camp educational experience, we make three assumptions.

1. The ministry of the church to youth in a wilderness setting can meet educational objectives in a theological framework that may not be experienced in the traditional Sunday church school or even in the traditional church camp.

2. A close, group-living experience for an extended period of time (five to seven days), supported by a minimum of cultural conveniences, can provide a uniquely productive environment in which youth and adults can grapple together with basic questions of life (Who am I? Who is God? etc.).

3. The participants in a wilderness experience may come more quickly to appreciate their resources, both within themselves and in the world around them, than they might in a classroom setting.

Responding to these assumptions forces an evaluation of contemporary Christian education programming in all areas of the church's ministry to youth. This is necessary in order to determine the potential values of wilderness Christian education. My experience and the resulting observations may help the reader to formulate more clearly his or her approach to the exciting values of a wilderness-based Christian education program.

What we are after is not innovative change merely for the sake of doing something different. We are after a quality of ministry that will enhance the educational program of the church. The ultimate test of the educational program is how well it helps each individual develop and use his or her unique talents and how it meets his or her needs.

The thrust of this manual will be directed toward the needs of youth and how the church can minister most effectively to those needs. As the young person passes, "gradually but persistently, from the higher personal family envelope to the eminently impersonal societal envelope . . . . we witness the steady arousal of affective responses to social, moral, and spiritual issues."[3] What happens in the initial stage of adolescence has a marked effect on the subsequent total development of the adolescent. When the church has the opportunity to make a contribution to this development, that opportunity must be taken very seriously. It demands our best effort.

The ministry to adolescents through wilderness trail camping is an attempt to provide activities and interaction patterns which can help to resolve many of the pain-producing conflicts of the adolescent. The relatively large block of time devoted to relationships, contrasted with the shorter blocks of time generally available in other forms of ministry, contributes greatly to the effectiveness of wilderness Christian education. The smallness of the group and the intimacy of the counselor/camper relationships increase the expectations for openness, making it much easier to run the risk of sharing personal needs or to grapple thoroughly with a problem in seeking its solution. These intimate personal contacts and the growing trust relationships are almost as essential as life itself. Providing the opportunity for these important contacts and relationships puts a stamp of validity upon the ministry of wilderness trail camping. It also makes a strong case for using this kind of youth ministry as a viable means of Christian education.

"The biblical patterns of 'a people on the way' pictures a team approach, people banded together for a common cause."[4] Wilderness trail camping reflects that pattern. Active participation is essential for the well-being of the group. Cooperative involvement becomes the strength of the group and finds its exemplar in the biblical narrative. The validity of Christian education comes only as it is in process—on the way to that which God intends: the Promised Land, the new Jerusalem, the new person in Christ.

The freedom of relationships—with all that this means in terms of independency and interdependency, the opportunity to explore the meaning of self, others, God, and the natural world—is in keeping with the biblical image of humankind in motion, struggling to be free. The out-of-doors provides a natural counterpart to the biblical rationale for ministry. If the biblical patterns are to be meaningfully related to our lives, somehow those patterns must reach the inner recesses of our lives. There is no better way for this to happen than through experience-centered education which is thoroughly immersed in the biblical process.

When one comes to any biblical study of wilderness, what immediately comes to mind is God's basic action in the wilderness with the people of Israel. The wilderness experience provided Israel with a creed preserving the fundamental events of God's unique dealings with them. That creed became the significant foundation for the Judeo-Christian tradition.

If we want to discover with our youth what it means to be Christian, if we want to discover with them the theological elements encompassed by being Christian, then we will involve ourselves with them in a community of faith in an environment where the greatest opportunities are available for making these discoveries. In addition, we will seek out an environment where there will be the least distractions from our quest. We will deliberately expose ourselves to the kinds of experiences and interactions with them which allow the greatest freedom in coming to grips with an understanding of self, others, and God. If possible, we will seek the maximum exposure to an intensive learning situation because

> through . . . concentrated educational experiences in which some of the needs of searching faith—intellectual inquiry, action, and experimentation in community—are met, persons can be nurtured in the expansion of their faith.[5]

The ministry to adolescents through wilderness trail camping is uniquely equipped to provide theologically relevant answers which will satisfy some of the needs of young people searching for faith.

Answers like these are not the product of rote learning. Carl Rogers defines such learning as "learning which takes place 'from the neck up.' It does not involve feelings or personal meanings; it has no relevance for the whole person."[6] Contrast this with significant, meaningful experiential learning.

> For example, while undergoing experiences such as meeting all kinds of weather, preparing his own food, and living and working with [persons of divergent backgrounds], the camper comes to realize that his own comfort is directly related to others and how much he must respect the

rights of the other campers. Meeting the hardships of the out-of-doors often turns out to be enjoyable and leaves vivid impressions of human values.[7]

The emotional impact of certain experiences may be of far greater importance than the value that may accrue from a carefully worded explanation. The wilderness approach to Christian teaching may include words, the symbols of reality; it will also include the involvement of the senses, possibly at an emotional or feeling level never before experienced.

Those of us with a keen interest in the future of the church's ministry in wilderness education have the responsibility of selecting those teaching methods which have shown promise and which have potential for continually expanding the educational ministry. The ministry to youth through wilderness trail camping has begun to accumulate sufficient data to warrant its future use as a viable teaching arm of the church. The future of wilderness Christian education will be as strong as our commitment to, and use of, the biblical, theological, and pedagogical rationale for this ministry.

Part I.

The Value of Wilderness Christian Education

As I have participated in workshops for persons interested in the ministry of trail camping, I have discovered that an alarming number of persons, when asked to respond to the question, "Why do you want to have a part in this trail-camping experience?" are hard pressed to answer in a theoretical vein. Quite often the answer is couched in terms from an experience-oriented perspective: "I like to get out into the out-of-doors"; "I want to see kids have a good time in the mountains"; "I was given a new backpack, and it needs to see some use!"; "They needed another counselor and here I am."

Honest responses; but if trail camping is to provide a viable means of experiential education from a Christian perspective, there must be some understanding of the theoretical dynamics underlying the practical experience. To put it another way, we must come to grips with an understanding of the theory that provides meaning and purpose for the experience.

In chapter 1, I will share my interpretation of wilderness. I will also offer a philosophy of wilderness camping which supports the educational aspects of a creative Christian ministry with youth. Chapter 2 will provide a physical, social, psychological, and religious perspective of adolescence, with a view toward meeting these needs through wilderness education. In chapter 3 I will discuss the spiritual value of the wilderness experience, specifically as this is revealed in the biblical narrative. This section concludes with an assessment of the strengths and weaknesses of wilderness experiential education.

Chapter 1

Wilderness Experiential Education: A Christian Perspective

From my tower study window I can gaze across the miles to the beauty of the snow-covered slopes of Mount Baker, standing majestically against the backdrop of the rugged North Cascades of Washington. The view of the mountains is beautiful indeed! But the real thrill of knowing a mountain, regardless of its locale, comes only when we accept the challenge to plant our feet upon its forest-covered and snowfield-ornamented terrain.

When encountered firsthand, the flowing contours of the timbered slopes become a multidimensional conglomerate of shaded glens and flower-studded meadows. Mountainsides that seem gentle at a distance can become impassable ridges or steep grades that tax one's physical stamina to the limit. Even the inviting, smooth snowfields withdraw their welcome mat as the wilderness traveler approaches. The hiker discovers not smooth slopes but rather acres and acres of jumbled blocks of ice and snow interlaced with yawning crevasses.

The wilderness is wild—rugged—dangerous—breathtakingly beautiful—challenging—rewarding—close to the heart of God—and it must be experienced to be appreciated fully! The visitor to the wilderness must be prepared to rise to the challenges of its resplendent, yet sometimes hostile, environment. The ill-equipped intruder, lacking adequate food, shelter, and clothing, may rue the day he or she set foot within its domain. The wilderness draws us away from the realm of our own accomplishments and brings us close to the unspoiled majesty of God's creative handiwork. Here the simplicity of life encourages us to rethink our values and reexamine our goals in living.

The wilderness experience can provide the hardships, challenges, and encounters with the unknown which test our mettle, calling forth responses that result in personal maturity and rewarding growth. As we allow our spiritual sensitivities to regain their sharpness, a sharpness often blunted by a capitulation to the sometimes overwhelming pressures of a sophisticated society, something refreshing happens. If we, like Elijah, will step outside of the "caves" in our lives, which contain our precious memorabilia of time clocks, agendas, appointments, and deadlines, we may be pleasantly startled as we hear the still, small voice of God! (1 Kings 19:13).

I am convinced that the wilderness can be used meaningfully as a vehicle for Christian experiential education. The change of pace, the change of approach from more traditional patterns, provides an environment of relaxed informality which allows more time for participants to interrelate in an atmosphere of freedom. This allows the necessary ingredients of growth—thinking, exploring, questioning, and discovering answers—to surface meaningfully. The preceding influences and ingredients of growth, combined with the responsible leadership of Christians effectively modeling their faith, can facilitate personal and spiritual growth for each individual.

WHY WILDERNESS?

What does the wilderness have to offer as a vehicle of Christian education that makes it unique as far as the church is concerned? Let's look more carefully into the question. It is a good one and must be adequately answered before we can even begin to develop a philosophy of wilderness Christian education.

Wilderness defined.

It is amazing how difficult it is to find a definitive interpretation of "wilderness." Most are experience-oriented and others are quite poetical. "Wilderness is the America that was . . . wilderness is fragile." [1] Another writer suggests that it is a place "where you can be serene, that will let you contemplate and connect two consecutive thoughts, or that if need be can stir you up as you were meant to be stirred up, until you blend with the wind and water and earth you almost forgot you came from." [2]

The definition of wilderness, as expressed in the Wilderness Act of 1964, deserves attention. It is "an area where the earth and its community of life are untrammeled by man, where man himself is a visitor who does not remain." [3] Biblically, the meaning of wilderness is "desert," representing a hostile environment. It was a place of temptation and involved a time for testing. It symbolized the interval between bondage and freedom. Something of that meaning was picked up by the early frontiersman. Wilderness was an adversary to be conquered, an environment to be subdued, changed, and tamed. Since the time of Thoreau, when wilderness began to be seen as an aesthetic environment to be appreciated, it has become less fearful and more enjoyable.

Wilderness is an essence, as well as geographical reality, that has had to struggle to be recognized and appreciated. In our technologically oriented society we have been tempted to bring everything under human control. If some particular place of exquisite natural beauty has been discovered, our first impulse seems to be to make it as easily accessible as possible, as soon as possible. Witness the human overkill of Yosemite Valley!

In determining suitable locations for wilderness trail camping, we will consider the criterion that it be land set apart and designated as a wilderness area by government regulations. This means that there will be no roads into the area nor any mechanized means of transportation permitted. Wilderness land will be in its native state, untouched by any so-called civilized improvements. Admittedly (and fortunately) there are some areas outside of designated wilderness reserves that could qualify as a wilderness area by this definition.

Wilderness as experience.

A sense of the experiencing of wilderness will help us in arriving at a clearer definition of wilderness. At the same time it will move us closer to an answer to our original question concerning the uniqueness of wilderness as a vehicle of Christian education.

It seems that there are at least two major components of the wilderness experience. First of all, there is the joy and exhilaration of being there: "the experience (to use Thoreau's words) of being refreshed 'by the sight of inexhaustible vigor,' of being emotionally overwhelmed by the vast and titanic forces of nature."[4] It is the experience of climbing up switchbacks in the shelter of old growth forests, then suddenly breaking into a fragile mountain meadow, and, while looking up at the surrounding rugged crags and snow-covered vistas, gasping out in amazement at the incredible beauty God has provided.

Recognizing that a similar type of experience might be attainable while motoring through the mountains in the comfort and convenience of the family car, we must mention the second, and possibly more important, component of the wilderness experience. This has to do with the whole process of *how* we arrive at the scene of our emotional and spiritual reward. "The exquisite sight, sound, and smell of wilderness is many, many times more powerful if it is earned through physical achievement, if it comes at the end of a long and fatiguing journey for which vigorous good health is a necessity."[5] I like the way one trail camper expressed it in his log book:

> Well, today we went up those treacherous switchbacks. Zooosh! When you go up those things you have just enough strength to take the next step. Just when you think you've had it, a nice cool wind blows, or you see a good view and stop and catch your breath; or you come to a small stream to dip your head in a couple of times!

The struggle that must be experienced by those who opt for the wilderness experience is a very real part of the definition of wilderness. Wilderness must be remote. It must be beyond the "edge of civilization." It must not be easily attained. Elements of this philosophy have meaning for the educational process. Easy achievement can be the downfall of our educational system. Quality growth most often occurs in the face of difficulty. Christian educators can utilize the rigors of the wilderness experience to encourage and facilitate Christian maturity in our youth.

Wilderness as involvement.

The wilderness experience offers involvement on a more intense scale than the traditional classroom experience, or even the site-camp experience. There are no spectators on the trail-camping venture. Survival requires involvement. Each participant is responsible for seeing that the necessities of living are met each day—from the fixing of meals and setting up camp for the night to transporting himself or herself and his or her belongings along the trail. Teamwork is vital to the successful outcome of the wilderness experience as each person contributes strengths to the group and draws on the strengths of others where he or she is weak.

The wilderness lures us away from our familiar, fast-paced world and brings us in touch with the matchless creation of almighty God. Living together in this environment enables us to think about our values and to focus on the basic issues of direction for our lives. Here, too, is the opportunity to explore and practice Christian living in a very close and intense twenty-four-hour-a-day living situation with others. The wilderness commands discipline and respect from those who would appreciate it, and at the same time can teach reverence for the omnipotent, omniscient, and omnipresent Creator and Savior. A camper writes,

> Possibly the biggest temptation of this week is merely to exist and make it through rather than experiencing the lessons to be learned. The aching muscles, sore feet, and rain can get me down, but perhaps this is another opportunity to live above the circumstances—focusing on the fact that God loves me and really understands and cares how I'm feeling.

Wilderness as freedom.

Another unique quality of the wilderness is the comparative freedom from a rigorous time schedule. The sun rises and sets to be sure, but no five-minute warning or annoying clanging of the bell signals the end of the class period! It won't hurt to leave your watch back in civilization. If you have ever taught in a classroom situation, you can probably admit that more than once time has controlled or manipulated you—and the students—as you pursued some goal in your lesson plan. No bell will halt abruptly a learning activity in the wilderness setting before you reach a satisfactory completion point.

Wilderness and creativity.

Perhaps the greatest incentive to use the wilderness as a vehicle for Christian education is found in the limitless creativity it affords. Jesus was a creative teacher. The lessons he impressed upon people's minds by directing their attention to the natural world are legion and still speak to us today. "Jesus tried to understand what people were thinking and pushed them to think more deeply, more honestly, more searchingly, more penetratingly, and more constructively."[6] The people of Jesus' day faced obstacles which needed to be overcome if they were to behave creatively and respond with appropriate religious faith. Young people who participate in our trail camps still struggle with these same obstacles. Can you picture the young person who wrote, "What an afternoon! My attitude was as bad as I felt physically—lousy. I was hot, tired, and my feet were killing me." Later, that same person would write "I'm learning to love people when they rub me the wrong way. It really hurts now to learn this (my attitude was horrible!). I must be bullheaded. I'm forgiven though, and I'm thankful that God is teaching me something. Now maybe I can love anyone, no matter what." Reflective utilization of teachable moments in the wilderness setting will encourage one toward becoming a mature person in Christ.

Wilderness as learning environment.

The very nature of the wilderness experience quickly creates an atmosphere of mutual trust, respect, helpfulness, freedom of expression, and acceptance of differences. These can also be experienced in other settings, but when the welfare of the total group is at stake, they come about more quickly. This situation makes for a true learning environment.

On one particularly difficult camp (junior high), when the weather absolutely refused to cooperate, we were faced with crucial decisions several times. Because heavy rain had forced us to postpone our camp by one day, the group opted to bypass a possible campsite. This meant hiking an additional three miles to reach the Cascade crest on a trail recently hiked by the trail leader. Options for camping were available should anyone in the group have found the hike too tiring. The youth responded splendidly and had a great sense of accomplishment in conquering a total of seven miles and gaining 2,600 feet in elevation! Upon our arrival at the campsite, the combined effect of rain, fog, wind, and cold made us aware of the very real danger of hypothermia. Precamp briefing on the effects of hypothermia facilitated the important decision to provide shelter and warm food in record time. Everyone pitched right in! On the final day we had to break camp early because of the weather, repeating the seven-mile hike, downhill this time, first through snow (in August!) and then in heavy rain at the lower elevations.

In retrospect, one junior-high participant summed it all up in this way:

Looking back on the week, I can't say that if I had the chance to do the same again—that I would do it. I don't regret any of it, though. Everyone got along so well and was so willing to help the other guy out. I think that in spite of the wind, rain, snow, and freezing cold weather, everyone would say that it was a very rewarding week, not only because of the sights that were seen, but because of the friendships that started and *grew* throughout the entire week. Everything was great!!!

A counselor added these words,

The value in the uncontrolled hardships and limited reflecting and talking time was that these led to camper unity and cooperation.

With civilized conveniences stripped away and our activities dictated by the weather, the true picture of our necessities (shelter, warmth, food, fellowship) became clearer, and it was evident how God met these needs for us.

When everyone is involved and each one is willing to "accept responsibility for planning and operating the learning experience, [then] there will be a mutual feeling of commitment to its success."[7] By becoming actively involved in the process, each can contribute freely from his or her experience. The important skill of making a full response to a new situation, or a new response to an old situation, is quickly sharpened within the wilderness framework of Christian education.

WILDERNESS CAMPING PHILOSOPHY

It might be safe to say that there are almost as many philosophies of camping as there are trails leading into the back country! At the same time, I know of no statement of philosophy that has been drawn up exclusively for Christian wilderness camping. Ask someone why she or he shoulders a pack and heads for the hills, and expect any answer ranging from "because I like to hike" to "I want to get away from a 'depersonalized, overpopulated, plastic, mechanized, unnatural, hectic, paved-over, materialistic, money-grubbing, boxed-in, uptight, artificial, over-regulated hassle.'"[8]

I know from my own explorations of the philosophy of church camping, and this includes site camps as well as trail camps, that much can be said relative to church camping that also applies to the philosophy of the church school. What my experience has convinced me of is simply this: we have not yet begun to tap the exciting potential of wilderness trail camping! A program for reaching and enabling young Christians through trail ministries can be as effective as we are capable of designing it to become! I believe it is a twentieth-century tool waiting to be pressed into service by the church and can be utilized by the Holy Spirit to become an effective means of developing promising participants in the body of Christ.

As we approach the wilderness, we may have the image of a Daniel Boone or a John Muir in our minds. In reality, we will be setting our specially-designed-for-hiking boots on well-graded forestry-service trails (usually), and on our backs we will have the latest equipment designed by space-age technology—created from ultra-light aluminum and rip-stop nylon. So much the better for us. We will have eased the danger of our own physical collapse—most of us are not as rugged as a Boone or a Muir—and we will be able to devote more time to the pursuit of our spiritual and educational objectives.

The value of church camps as a means of providing spiritual, educational, and *physical* enrichment was first explored around 1880. Reverend George W. Hinkley, desiring to know some of the boys in his church better as well as encourage them to a closer relationship with God, took them on a camping trip in that year. About the same time, Reverend H. H. Murray, pastor of Park Street Church in Boston, established the first church camp. He "is regarded by many as the father of the great outdoor movement from which the camping movement sprang." [9]

Down through the years there has been a veritable procession of experiences which, by design or happenstance, have been the attempts of the church to capture the spirit of the out-of-doors for use in its program of spiritual nurture. Some of these became the "camp-meeting"—eventually conference-type programs. The comfort of padded chairs in cathedral-like assembly halls reached by concrete or asphalt walkways that wind their way from adequately furnished "cabins" seems scarcely removed from downtown living. God's voice in nature is seldom heard above the booming public address system or the whirring of tape recorders in the "teaching" sessions!

A secular perspective.

We can learn from the devotees of camping who have approached the experience from a nonreligious perspective. Sigurd Olson, who early in this century lived in the wilderness and served as a guide for others seeking the wilderness experience, writes:

> . . . something happened to men when they went into the bush. As they shed their city habits and settled down to the hard physical work and simplicity of primitive living, they laughed more and took pleasure in little things. Men who had not watched a sunset or a moonrise for years suddenly found such phenomena thrilling. They listened to the winds and the sounds of the forest, and the roar of the rapids lulled them to sleep. Men who had not looked at a flower, a bird, or a squirrel for a long time were not too busy any more for such pleasures. I once saw a business magnate engrossed for over an hour watching an ant hill, a man who until then had counted any moment lost that was not devoted to making money. Such things, I saw, became important as soon as men were removed from the complexities and responsibilities of the lives they had left. [10]

If we can capture something of the philosophy inherent in these experiences we will begin to crystallize our own thoughts toward a meaningful philosophy of wilderness Christian education. I believe such a philosophy must be a functional systêm of values derived from involvement in the wilderness experience. John Dewey's philosophy of education held education to be life, growth, social process, and reconstruction of experience.[11]

Wilderness is down-to-earth experience.

The wilderness experience is certainly not appropriate for those who prefer an ivory-tower approach to life. Even if it were possible to accumulate a headful of facts about wilderness *life,* the individual would not know—would not be educated to—what wilderness *living* is all about. The wilderness trail camp provides a miniature democratic society where youth may become naturally involved in education involving life, growth, social process, and reconstruction of experience. What they remember may well be what Olson's wilderness visitors remembered:

> What stayed with them was the good feeling after a day of tough portages or fighting some gale, the joy of warmth and food after exposure and reaching an objective under their own power. . . . most of all was the silence and the sense of removal. These were the spiritual dividends, hard to explain, impossible to evaluate, that brought them back time and time again. . . . what they really came for was to experience the deep and abiding satisfactions of primitive living under natural conditions.[12]

The spiritual dividends which Olson mentions have their parallel in the wilderness Christian education program. Indeed, they are at the heart of what takes place in the camp that is sensitive to the spiritual dynamic. They appear when education and experience fuse.

> Very little may be said about spiritual values in words, but they will be communicated if they are present in the spirit of the leaders, in their motives for being at camp, in their vision of goals, and in their sensitivity for helping campers have worthy goals of their own that may be achieved by engaging in delightful activities.[13]

Sometimes the activities of a trail camp are anything but delightful. There are times when wilderness campers may find that the activities are extremely difficult, perhaps even painful, but in experiencing the difficulties and the pain, they learn indelible lessons! I chuckled as a counselor commiserated about the toughness of the trail and then pensively stated, "I wonder how Jesus felt as he made his wilderness journey—but he had the advantage of not having to carry a pack!"

Further reflection upon the ability of Jesus to discern God's will even in moments of extreme physical weakness proved to be a learning moment as a biblical truth fused with real-life experience.

Focus on experiential education.

This link of education and experience is a "must" in striving for viable results from the wilderness education experience. Learning by doing is the goal of most educators, but, unfortunately, many times we are hampered by our surroundings. This can be especially true in a classroom situation, locked into rows of chairs confined by four walls. The wilderness sets us free! Here we do not merely show or tell our youth about an experience, we encourage them to *live* the experience.

One of the keys to experiential learning lies in consciously reflecting upon a given experience and then drawing relevent lessons from the experience. The lesson might focus upon a new appreciation for one's physical capabilities. A young man who is proud of his ability to perform thirty push-ups exudes a totally new and satisfying concept of himself when he stands with his pack on a hard-won ridge and says, "I did it! I really did it!"

With all of our concern for planet earth, the real lesson of responsibility seems more comprehensible as youth observe the impact which they themselves make upon a fragile environment. Is it possible to care for a campsite in such a way that the next campers who stop will wonder how long it has been since someone used the area? Will the lesson penetrate deeply enough so that care of one's environment becomes a way of life?

I consider it a compliment to the integrity of wilderness camping when parents inform me that their youth have returned from the experience with a more serious, thoughtful, appreciative, and enthusiastic attitude toward life. It is even more satisfying when an observable spiritual maturation has taken place, signaling a fresh new sensitivity to what God is all about in our world.

Kurt Hahn, known as the father of Outward Bound (an outdoor education program), developed his program out of a felt need to engender enthusiasm and social responsibility in young people by developing their mental alacrity, physical well-being, and pride in accomplishment through experiences which involved tremendous physical stress.[14] The results of this philosophy have been impressive. An example from World War II days tells of Louis Holt, the owner of a line of British merchant ships, who was concerned over the many young sailors who were succumbing to the rigors of survival in a life boat after being torpedoed at sea. Older men, in the same situation, had a better survival rate apparently because they had already endured other stress situations related to a less sophisticated style of life than that enjoyed by the younger men. Holt heard of Dr. Hahn's Outward Bound program, and commissioned him to start a school in Wales. The remarkable result was that the young apprentice seamen who went through the controlled experience of the school and learned to cope with stress had a greater rate of survival.[15]

In further developing this philosophy of learning by doing, a core of basic premises can be formulated. (1) The birthright of every youth includes familiarity with the natural environment. (2) An understanding of social relationships, such as those developed in close in-group living on the trail, is essential to growth. (3) Understanding what happens to the group when the individual exercises the right of freedom of choice and self-determination is part of the maturation process. (4) Basic skills in caring for oneself and others are essential. (5) Identification and exercise of appropriate attitudes toward authority and responsibility in a democratic framework are a must. Additionally, all the preceding premises can achieve their ultimate meaning for the Christian life-style when the intimate relationships of group living create situations in which the campers are helped to understand and practice the teachings of Jesus.

The coeducational camp.

The question of whether to have a coeducational trail camp or a single-sex camp is a question that can be related to the philosophy of the camp leadership. I have conducted coeducational wilderness camps as well as all male wilderness camps with both junior and middle high youth, and I prefer the coeducational experience. Actually pioneered by church groups, the coeducational camp "provides a much more realistic approach to personal growth. It is particularly important in dealing with young adolescents that both sexes learn to understand each other and to work together."[16]

Regardless of gender, young people have hopes, aspirations, and desires that are very similar. They have a strong drive to belong; they want to be respected; they want to have friends. In the coeducational camp these needs can be met by others of the same sex as well as by those of the opposite sex. The presence of both sexes in a camp may have the desired effect of stabilizing the overall group. Christian education goals are more quickly met when there is a settled attitude in the wilderness camp.

Implementing a philosophy reflecting the dynamics of living in the wilderness does not just happen. Advance planning by the leader and counselors is imperative to insure that a well-organized pattern of activities will bring to life the purposes of the trail-camp experience and achieve the desired results. The results should reflect the purpose derived from the philosophy of those who planned the wilderness camping experience.

WILDERNESS CHRISTIAN EDUCATION

Individuals who have a genuine interest in bringing values from the disciplines of theology, psychology, sociology, and anthropology into effective Bible study in a meaningful way have developed the following statement of objective shared by a number of denominations:

> The goal of the church's educational ministry is that all persons be aware of God through God's self-disclosure, especially God's redeeming love as revealed in Jesus Christ, and, enabled by the Holy Spirit, respond in faith and love, that as new persons in Christ they may know who they are and what their human situation means, grow as children of God rooted in the Christian community, live in obedience to the will of God in every relationship, fulfill their common vocation in the world, and abide in the Christian hope.[17]

I believe that wilderness Christian education is an integral part of the church's educational ministry, sharing the objective as stated above. Wilderness Christian education is a specialized facet of the ministry of church camping which is part of the total program of Christian education in the church, including both children and adults. The intense nature of the twenty-four-hour-a-day experience of camping gives it the potential of being one of the most meaningful parts of the total Christian education program. Isolation and freedom from an artificial environment, added to the time involvement, make wilderness camping an even more all-encompassing experience.

The importance of clarity in stating objectives.

As a new ministry develops, it is imperative that its objectives be stated clearly and understood. I believe that only after this is done will the program and materials of wilderness Christian education rise to the heights of their potential. This new potential is exciting in light of the observation that the foundations of Christian education are being tested.

Wilderness Christian education is a fresh new possibility for a model that can make a clean break from the idea that we must have some sort of "school" as the context for our educational procedure as well as some form of instruction as the means. As creatures of habit, we may subconsciously carry that model into the wilderness in our heads! At the same time we must not throw the baby out with the bath water.

I have already stated that the objective of wilderness Christian education ought to be in complete accord with the objective of our denominational ministries. The fresh wind of change—that might also infuse new life into the prevailing programs of the church—is the awareness that teaching which simply *implants* knowledge in the mind of the learner is woefully inadequate when compared to teaching that permits the learner to *experience* knowledge.

The Christian education objective indicates that regardless of where the church's teaching ministry is expressed, in a classroom, at a site camp, or in the wilderness, that ministry is concerned about our fundamental and universal questions: "Who am I?" "Why am I here?" "Who is my neighbor?" It also indicates that the answers to these questions find their ultimate meaning when we come to the knowledge of God. The Christian life is a relationship, beginning with a basic relationship in God. How we relate to others will be conditioned by the validity of that basic relationship, a validity that begins when we encounter God's self-disclosure in Jesus Christ. The objective also recognizes that there is something beyond the present moment of experience. The Christian struggles daily with change, always aware through the ministry of the Holy Spirit that present imperfections can be exchanged for something better—ultimately the resurrection life with God beyond death.

The basic concerns of wilderness Christian education.

The objectives, then, of wilderness Christian education are to bring the camper to a growing awareness of God; to encourage a meaningful relationship to God through Jesus Christ; to provide for incisive self-acceptance and understanding; to develop meaningful relationships with others, grounded in love; and to enable a growing attitude of hope, both in this life and in its ultimate fulfillment in life beyond death.

It is interesting to note how often in the Bible the wilderness was that unique environment used for a place of refuge, and at the same time a place where the individual could be ministered to by God and prepared for some specific ministry.

The present-day wilderness traveler will find that

> the aesthetic beauty, the deep appreciation for nature, the feeling of complete humbleness, the wonderment, the pondering, the full trust and belief, the joy, the complete relaxation, the simplicity, the complexity, the magnitude, the relationships, the belongings, all are a part of the intellectual, emotional, and spiritual learning that comes as a result of a direct experience with nature.[18]

Intellectual, emotional, and spiritual learning can serve only as introductory steps to a personal knowledge of God. To stop short of that actual experience is to miss the mark of the basic objective of Christian education. "We are not saved by our knowledge, our beliefs, or our worship . . . just as we are not saved by our actions or our religion. We are saved by the anguish and love of God. . . ."[19] The wilderness Christian educator will want to make the most of experiences that open the heart and mind of the camper to come to grips with the anguish and love of God.

I found an illustration for this on a wild and cold stormy night at a remote, lakeside campsite. Shrieking gusts of wind accompanied with the sound of crashing branches from surrounding trees drove all thought of sleep from my mind. I had to double-check my campers to make sure no one had pitched a tent in a vulnerable location. I was able to crawl back into the warmth and security of my tent only after I had ascertained that the rest of the group was secure. The thought of even one young person being in danger was frightening. The incident recalled the awareness Jesus had of a shepherd's concern for his sheep with the corresponding message that God's love and anguish could not tolerate the thought of "one of these little ones" perishing (Matthew 18:6-14).

Goals of wilderness Christian education.

In harmony with the objective of wilderness Christian education, there are certain goals to be kept in our minds as we teach in the wilderness.[20] Basic to these goals is a desire to see a value-loaded quality of Christian life develop rather than an assembly-line product bearing certain evidence of fixed beliefs or codes of behavior. The assembly-line product of our teaching may be an educated atheist!

Goal One: Attitudes

Philippians 2:5 states that we are to have the mind of Christ in us. This is a part of the process of becoming new persons in Christ. It presents the goal of developing an attitude toward God and ourselves based on love. Loving God and loving others as we love ourselves will bring to us an awareness that must touch the whole of life. Wilderness living will present many opportunities to experience how love can be felt, shown, and nurtured. Several of our boys, carrying the pack of a woman counselor who was briefly ill on the trail, became an object lesson in attitude that was not soon forgotten. As a discussion point in the educational process, further insights were elicited from the campers. Moments of insight can be nurtured into a chosen life-style which will seek to reflect the attitude of Christ.

Goal Two: Relationships

Love practiced in isolation must be purely academic. It is only as we relate to other human beings that we begin to understand what love and respect for other persons means. It is also the way in which we begin to grasp and understand how God works in our lives, in the lives of others, and through our lives to one another. The importance of attitude that surfaced when the campers took turns carrying a disabled person's pack resulted in bringing the total trail group together in a depth of relationship that could not have been brought about at that depth of intensity in the schooling-instructional paradigm! The development of caring and mutual trust will result in campers reaching toward maturity in Christ.

Goal Three: Content

Knowing who we are, growing as children of God, living in obedience, fulfilling our common vocation, and abiding in Christian hope should not come about simply because we have been *told* that these qualities are correct for the Christian. Too often the results may be purely academic. We need to learn how to examine data and then arrive at well-thought-through decisions. This process ought to be, and can be, an exciting and stimulating experience. It is one thing to be told that there is no water available on a five-mile section of trail on the south side of a mountain on a super-warm day; it is quite another thing to experience it! The value of a water bottle (filled, of course!), the best time of day to hike, the interpretive signs which indicate a spring are important data relative to arriving at a good decision. This simple illustration can be amplified into an exciting lesson for the seeker of spiritual truth. Content has to do with equipping campers to think things through rather than providing answers for them.

Goal Four: Ethics

Our understanding of the nature of God, our beliefs about the nature of human beings, and an awareness of our responsibility to the world of nature ought to encourage us toward sound principles of moral and

ethical education. We must grapple with a growing need for understanding how God intends human life to be lived in community and
how God intends for us to be responsible stewards of the world in
which we live. Wilderness Christian education must do more than *teach*
about goodness and responsibility. It must also involve practicing social
skills, living by the rules of the community, and caring for the resources
of the environment. Have you ever filled your drinking cup with water
from a fragile wilderness stream, only to discover a camper just upstream
washing out his dirty socks? I promise that you will not lack for
experience-related teaching moments on a wilderness camping experience!

Secular camping objectives.

The following objectives of camping from a secular perspective
provide affirmation of what I have written thus far. The wilderness
leader would do well to correlate these with his or her understanding
of the Christian education goals for the wilderness experience:

1. The development of a sense of "at-home-ness" in the natural world and
   the art of outdoor living.
   a) Increased understanding and appreciation of the world of nature.
   b) A keener sense of responsibility for the conservation of natural resources.
   c) Understanding of man's dependence on nature.
   d) Ability to use basic camping skills.
2. Education for safe and healthful living.
   a) Ability to use basic camping skills.
   b) Improve eating habits and nutritional status.
   c) Increased vitality, endurance and strength.
   d) The formation of positive health habits.
   e) Adjustment to physical defects.
   f) Safety skills indigenous to the out-of-doors.
   g) Freedom from mental tensions.
3. Education for constructive use of leisure.
   a) Ability to camp with ease.
   b) Development of a variety of skills useful in adult life.
   c) Creative ability in developing recreational activities.
   d) Increased understanding and appreciation of the out-of-doors.
4. Contribution to personality development.
   a) Development of increased self-reliance and initiative.
   b) Adjustment to physical defects.
   c) Development of various skills.
   d) Increased creative ability.
   e) Freedom from parental control.
   f) A sense of worth as an individual through belonging to a group.

    g) Development of ability to analyze, judge, make intelligent decisions.
    h) Freedom from mental tension.
    i) An appreciation of comradeship.
    j) Ability to cooperate and be considerate of others.
    k) A sense of social understanding and responsibility.
    l) An understanding and appreciation of persons of other religions, cultures, nationalities, races.
    m) A sense of kinship with and security in an orderly universe.
5. Education for democratic group and individual living.
    a) Understanding of our pioneer heritage.
    b) A sense of worth as an individual.
    c) Development of ability to analyze, judge, make decisions.
    d) Ability to cooperate and think of others.
    e) A sense of social understanding and responsibility.
    f) Ability to function effectively in a democratic society.
    g) An understanding of the worth of every individual.
6. The development of spiritual meanings and values.
    a) An understanding and appreciation of persons of other religions, cultures, nationalities and races.
    b) A deeper sense of religious values as expressed in all phases of living.
    c) A sense of kinship with the security in an orderly universe.
    d) A keener sense of aesthetic appreciation.[21]

Curriculum techniques.

Since so little prepared material is currently available in the area of wilderness Christian education curriculum, the wilderness leader must be prepared to develop his or her own materials, or adapt church school or site camp materials for use in the wilderness. In developing or adapting materials it is important to remember that a primary concern will be to have a curriculum that will make the most of the experiential aspects of the educational process. Keep in mind, then, the following techniques as you develop your curriculum.

Observation.

Consistent with the wilderness principle of developing habits of inquiring and discovering, rather than presenting campers with neatly preformed packages of knowledge, is the technique of observation. One of the unique values of wilderness Christian education is the opportunity afforded campers to see things in their natural setting and in relationship to other elements in their environment.

If you have ever noticed the beauty of the lupine flower, especially after a heavy dew or light rain, you have seen an instant object lesson. A droplet of water will collect at the junction of the leaves, giving the impression of a diamond nestling in the greenery. Jesus talked about flowers in the Sermon on the Mount and said "... even Solomon in all his glory was not arrayed like one of these." Many wilderness trails are luxuriously embellished with wildflowers of many shapes and colors, and the lessons drawn from them are legion. Observe how the avalanche lily seems to pursue the retreating snow. Notice that those which are several feet away from the snow are already completing their blooming cycle. "But if God so clothes the grass of the field, which today is alive and tomorrow is thrown into the oven, will he not much more clothe you, O men of little faith? Therefore do not be anxious ..." (Matthew 6:29-31). Make sure your curriculum encourages observation; then talk about what you see.

Investigation.

Commensurate with the technique of observation is the technique of investigation. In the wilderness, with the small teacher-student ratio, interested campers, and immediate contact with the world of nature, the principle of first-hand investigative experiences rises to its zenith. Wilderness Christian education abounds with experiences involving the use, enjoyment, and understanding of the wilderness environment.

A few of our campers, on a rather gloomy and threatening day weather-wise, took advantage of the layover day to investigate the slopes surrounding our camp. Poking around in the jumble of rocks, one of them discovered a chipmunk skull. This introduced an interesting discussion about the wildlife in the area—we had previously observed a doe in our camp—and ultimately led to a discussion with the counselor about Darwinism. Later, around the campfire the topic turned to death, perhaps triggered in the minds of the young people by the little skull. One of the girls, whose grandmother had died earlier in the year, shared some of her inner feelings, telling how God's love and strength had become real to her at a very difficult time. This sharing and the group's discussion later led one camper to write, "Tonight at our campfire we experienced closeness in the whole group for the first time." Make sure your curriculum encourages investigation. You may be surprised at the topics which ensue for the group's discussion!

Cooperation.

In the wilderness world members of the trail group are forced to take a close look at the dynamics of fellowship, appreciation and tolerance of others, and safety that occur in their hour-by-hour activities. Successful accomplishment of these dynamics requires cooperation. Without cooperative living the group will never become a true community.

Quite often in the wilderness a trail-camp group will come upon an obstacle in the trail that proves to be fairly difficult to overcome. It may be a particularly muddy bog or a stream where spring torrents have washed away the foot log. Regardless of the circumstances, group cooperation becomes a must. Packs may have to be taken off and passed along by hand. Campers may have to help one another over a fallen log. Sometimes a "human chain" is the best method for steadiness and security as a specially tricky spot in the trail is negotiated. Again, the experience provides a natural learning situation complete with the dynamics of fellowship, safety, and appreciation and toleration of others. Make the most of it by emphasizing cooperation in your curriculum.

Meditation.

One of the really helpful aspects of the wilderness experience, so conducive to the educational process, is the time available for meditation. Cultivate this technique. It is quite possible that there is no better time or place available to the camper to experience this educational technique than in the wilderness camping experience. Make the most of it. Provide ample time for meditation and contemplation so that all campers may share in the experience. The art of meditation will enrich the mind, the emotions, and the spirit.

When we stop to consider that the average young person has watched 20,000 hours of television by the time he or she is eighteen, it is quite reasonable to suspect that time for quiet meditation is a rare occurrence.[22] Television is only one of the many culprits vying for the attention of our minds, some with positive contributions to be made and many serving only to keep us from getting in touch with ourselves. I asked the youth on one of our trail camps to reflect on why they thought God revealed himself to Moses in the wilderness. The following comment pointed to one perceived value of wilderness as a good place for meditation: "I think God revealed himself to Moses in the wilderness because there, away from people, Moses and God could talk and be alone. I think God might reveal himself to us for similar reasons." Religiously, emotionally, intellectually, the technique of meditation is a valuable one.

Some additional techniques to be aware of as you prepare your curriculum for wilderness Christian education are informality, participation, and creativity.

Informality "does not mean that there is no organization, no plan. Actually, on the contrary, it frequently means that there is greater responsibility on the camper and certainly greater planning on the part of the leader.''[23] The informality of the wilderness experience can remove the struggle so often apparent in more formal settings.

Participation, with everyone involved (including the camper's input in the process of creating the learning situation), is one of the most helpful techniques in establishing the ideal learning situation. Participation connotes more than cooperation in that it carries the sense of an investment, buying into the process at the earliest possible moment. A well-designed curriculum involves leader and camper directly in the wilderness Christian education process.

We can find no better example than the ministry of Jesus for *creativity.* His teaching, underscored by authority, nonetheless captivated the hearts and minds of his hearers. He probed the imagination of those who listened; he involved them in the exploration of soul-freeing ideas; he helped them stretch to new dimensions of exciting living. We ought to attempt to do the same, and God's wilderness world is filled with lessons that can challenge our educational process to strive for the kind of creativity with which Christ taught!

Curriculum development.

Having looked at some of the goals, objectives, and techniques of wilderness Christian education, it will now be helpful to look at the process of developing the curriculum. The design that follows is based upon materials I have prepared and used in wilderness Christian education. The actual material printed for the campers' use is duplicated in Appendix A. Keep in mind that this is a suggested outline. Your wilderness leadership team will have an exciting time developing their materials once they get into the process.

Curriculum Title	**"Wilderness Lessons"**
Rationale	The wilderness provides varieties of experiences giving fresh insight to the wilderness camper in meeting his/her spiritual, social, psychological, mental, physical, and environmental awareness needs. These insights, coupled with illustrations from the Bible, encourage Christian growth and ecological sensitivity.
Description	Campers are encouraged to be aware of phys-

ical responses to the challenge of wilderness travel; to compare initial feelings with feelings that come as the week progresses. They will be challenged to become aware of the impact they make upon others, as well as understanding how their activities influence the environment. They will be stimulated to reflect upon how biblical lessons, in association with wilderness lessons, can enrich everyday living in the wilderness, as well as at home.

Purpose	To develop an increased awareness of the spiritual, social, psychological, mental, and physical dimensions of life with emphasis upon integrating insights into the totality of life as it is being experienced, including ecological responsibility.
Components	Input from Scriptures. Environmental responsibilities. Enabling from counselors. Reflection time. Small group interaction. Daily log.
Immediate goals	Improved attitudes toward self and others. Relationships reflecting a deeper understanding of love for self and others. A growing ability to perceive data and make a wise decision. A greater mindfulness in practicing social skills, living by the rules of the community, and caring for the resources of the environment.
Ultimate objectives	Being renewed in Christ, or becoming new persons in Christ, with increasing knowledge of who they are and how they relate to God, themselves, others, and the world.
Format	Leader-camper ratio will be one to three, or one to five depending on age level of camper. Materials needed are: devotional guide (see Appendix A), small notebook, and pen or

pencil. Five-day format adapts to the schedule of the camp. Leader can present overview
on initial day of camp. Group can share reflections on final day of camp.

SUMMARY AND CONCLUSION

I see a unique opportunity in wilderness trail camping for much
needed extension of the church's educational ministry into this field.
Experiential learning has great potential not only in the traditional
church-school and site-camp ministries but especially so in wilderness
trail camping. I am not saying that "all experiences are genuinely or
equally educative. Experience and education cannot be directly equated
to each other."[24] I am saying that the quality of the experience is all-
important. The ingredients are there in the wilderness environment for
a remarkable and valuable addition to the church's ministries. The key,
of course, lies in the leadership, and I will have more to say about that
in chapter 4.

Wilderness must be experienced to be appreciated. Reading about it
in books, viewing films, or even listening to others tell excitedly about
their experiences in the wilderness is not enough. One must *earn* the
privilege of enjoying the uplift, the exhilaration of being there. The
struggle sets the stage for quality experiences.

> Always when the struggle is real, when everyone's mettle is put to the
> utmost test, those who do their share are evident. Such [hikes] not only
> tighten one's muscles and firm one's decisiveness, they may be the means
> whereby, without a word being said by the counselor, some youngster
> turns from being a parasite to a puller, from being a leaner to a learner.[25]

A larch tree captured our attention one afternoon as we stood thirty
or forty feet above the shoreline of an exquisite jewel of an alpine
lake—a lake containing the clearest water one boy said he had ever
seen. The larch tree was almost directly across the lake from us. Its top
was nonexistent, smashed off repeatedly by the unbelievable power of
thunderous avalanches of snow. It was the lone survivor, standing
battered but proud in a hostile jungle of rock. We could not help
admiring all that it symbolized to us. Firmly it gripped the earth that
had given it birth. The worst that the elements could hurl upon it had
been shrugged off defiantly. Its presence there spoke of courage, te-
nacity, a will to live in the face of almost overwhelming odds. We
experienced a holy awe in viewing that tree and sensed that God was
bringing a vital lesson of life to us in a most creative way.

The responsibility of quality Christian education is not to be taken lightly. The uniqueness of the environment, the uniqueness of the individual, and the uniqueness of God's recreative purpose for each of us combine to present a provocative opportunity for ministry. Awareness of curriculum techniques will enable the wilderness leader to be sensitive to the physical and social surroundings and to utilize the surroundings in such a manner that the whole experience will be worthwhile. The wilderness leader will be aware of the inner resources as well as the spiritual dynamics which make unique contributions toward enabling the camper to become the person God desires each one to be.

Chapter 2

Understanding Adolescence: Guidelines for Involvement in Wilderness Education

Adolescence is a time of life without any really definitive age limits. It encompasses that period of life involving the transition from childhood to adulthood. A general overview of our society indicates that children ages eleven or twelve are close to the beginning of adolescence, initiating a period we will identify as early adolescence. Within several years the youth will be at the stage of development known as adolescence proper, usually associated with the middle-teen years. The next stage is called late adolescence and is the final period of physical, social, and psychological growth and adjustment prior to becoming an adult. It is important to remember that there are no hard and fast chronological age limits to any of these stages.

We are looking at a time of life when the individual is grappling with some of the most important developments that occur in the life cycle, developments that have to do with values, aspirations, roles, identity, and interaction patterns. Early adolescence is a crucial period in the life of the adolescent.

At this stage of life, what is happening in the world immediately around the early adolescent is extremely important to him or her. Individuals who constantly receive negative feedback from their interactions with others will have difficulty forming a positive self-image. Positive feedback, on the other hand, will do much to enhance the individual's sense of self-worth and will be reflected in his or her behavior patterns. Understanding how one person influences another individual as well as how the community affects individuals are important learning experiences for the adolescent.

The wilderness experience provides opportunity for small group community living in which the individual will be effectively removed, for a brief period, from the environmental and social situations that may be making an indelible negative impact upon his or her life. Efforts to be shallow or casual in relationship to this new environment and community do not stand up well; too much is at stake. Personal and group safety may depend upon how one relates to others; certainly the essence of community is affected—for good or ill—depending on the strength or weakness of individual self-images.

I found one young lad (in physical appearance he appeared to be the most mature camper in the group) in tears shortly after we had established camp the first night out on our wilderness journey. His complaint was that the other boys were hitting his tent with pieces of bark and small sticks. The incident was symptomatic of a shaky self-image. His physical size did not afford him automatic acceptance by the new community. A world that flowed quickly to his demands no longer surrounded him. His incongruent demands that his equipment be treated with respect not given to the equipment of others precipitated an encounter he could not handle. The week was a difficult one for this boy, but one hopes that he came away with some new insights into himself, as well as with a greater sense of the dynamics of the community of which he was a part.

This is not to say that society has a clear set of expectations for the adolescent. Certainly there are times when quite the opposite must appear to be the case. In certain situations the adolescent will be treated as a child; at other times the youth will be expected to respond as an adult. To complicate things further, an adult response will not necessarily bring adult privileges! The worker with adolescents, particularly very young adolescents, needs to be aware that psychologically the individual is still a child. This means that family, school, and society at large must "continue to extend their containing and protective roles, rather than push the young adolescent ahead under the misleading banner of 'the earlier and the faster, the bigger and the better.'"[1]

Early adolescents, regardless of size or shape, are very much caught up in the process of developing a sense of mastery. Basic school subjects keep them occupied, and motor-skill activities challenge their increasing capabilities. The early adolescent environment, "in its ideal form, is a flexible place where children in different stages of development can find what they need to help them grow."[2] The technological advances of our society tend to prolong the stages of adolescence by removing the pressures of a few generations ago when the young person was expected to take his or her place in specialized work responsibilities.

We need to capitalize on this and direct our ministry to the growth needs of adolescents.

The period of adolesence has some frustrating aspects for the young person, but it is also a time when he or she may experience a special tolerance from the adult world. "Adolescents are no longer considered to be children, and yet they are not really expected to take their position in the adult world. They have some adult privileges (status) but are not expected to take on full adult responsibilities (functions)."[3] The adolescent wilderness traveler is expected to shoulder (literally) his or her total survival supplies for the entire period of stay away from the comforts of civilization. The youth carries food, clothing, cooking gear, and other necessities for life in a backpack, just as the adults who accompany him or her. However, when a decision must be made between a dangerous shortcut across a treacherous snowslope or a much longer, snow-free route, that decision rests in the hands of a responsible adult with training and experience in making such decisions. I have had youth who loudly protested the decision not to cross the snowfield confess to me further along the trail, "I'm glad we didn't have to take that shortcut!" A later stop, near a snowfield with no dangerous slopes ending in a jumble of jagged rocks, can provide a training ground where youth and adults can practice snow-traveling skills safely and gain new insights into the dos and don'ts of this kind of travel.

It is sometimes necessary to override the exuberant and outwardly confident self-assurance of the adolescent because the physiological changes being experienced by the youth may affect his or her ability always to function rationally. Not understanding this phenomenon may cause the young person to experience frustration.

A brief overview of the adolescent—paying particular attention to physical, social, psychological, and religious development, as well as the relationship of the preceding to the process of the adolescent's becoming a mature person—will help us better understand how we might involve this age group effectively in wilderness Christian education.

PHYSICAL CHARACTERISTICS AND NEEDS OF THE ADOLESCENT

The dynamics at work in the initial stages of early adolescence are extremely influential in determining the ultimate course of the young person's life. Of major importance in the adolescent's developing self-concept is his or her early body image. This image is always present. Most adolescents are not only conscious of their bodies but can be intensely sensitive to the real or imagined effect that their body image is projecting to the world.

Just what is happening in the broad spectrum of physiological and anatomical changes taking place in the adolescent's body? Among other things, there are

> . . . the development of primary and secondary sex characteristics; changes in size, weight, body proportions, and muscular development; related changes in strength, coordination, and skill. In some adolescents these changes occur very slowly and may extend for as long as five or six years. In others the changes may take place much more rapidly and be completed in one or two years. A rapid spurt of growth, though within the normal range, is particularly likely to produce troublesome psychological reactions, for the youngster finds it difficult to cope with so much change in a short period of time.[4]

Sometimes when the adolescent engages in exercise, he or she will experience certain physical manifestations, noticeably increased heart rate and feelings of overwhelming fatigue. The experiencing of these can create intense anxiety in the mind of the young person. A lack of understanding of the physiological changes of pubescence, along with an extreme preoccupation with what one is "feeling," sets the stage for this anxiety. It is not uncommon to find an early adolescent, who, after a few miles on a wilderness trail, suddenly is convinced that "if I take another step, I'll die!" Given the assurance that a recent medical examination (required) has declared the camper fit, the wilderness leader can encourage the young person to keep going with appropriate rest periods and, in the process, learn to test—and stretch—his or her limits of endurance. The wilderness learning experience can help the adolescent resist a hypochondriacal preoccupation with his or her physical condition through this process of testing of physical capabilities.

Two major needs related to the adolescent's fast growth and development are food and rest. Calorie needs are enormous at the peak of the growth spurt. One of the reasons that the adolescent, especially a boy, seems always to be eating is that his stomach may be too small to hold the amount of food needed to meet the continuous demand for calories. Extra snacks will help meet this need. At the same time adequate rest must be encouraged to allow the body to cope with the demands being made upon it by the rapid physiological growth. The sensitive counselor learns to differentiate between genuine tiredness and an unwillingness to make an adequate effort.

Awareness of the dynamics of rapid growth is important in a ministry to adolescents, especially in wilderness trail camping. Bones, muscles, joints, and tendons are especially vulnerable to unusual strain as a result of the rapid growth. This fact mandates careful awareness of the types and intensity of physical involvement by the camper. Early adolescent boys, in particular, may be tempted to overexert themselves because of their awareness of increased strength and physical prowess. This awareness makes them susceptible to being egged on to the point of exhaustion. This introduces the social characteristic of peer pressure and the associated desire of an adolescent to win approval in the eyes of a peer group. More discussion will follow in the section on the social characteristics and needs of the adolescent.

The wilderness education program is in a unique position to make a valuable contribution toward meeting the physical needs of the adolescent. One way of doing this is by establishing sound principles of health care through promoting basic principles of good fitness. A good fitness program will develop stamina. One of the best activities for developing circulatory-respiratory endurance, simply because it involves continuous muscle exercise for thirty minutes and more, is wilderness hiking. Variation of pace, naturally caused by changes in terrain, also contributes to endurance development.

Educators are convinced that a sound physical body will provide definite benefits toward a healthy self-image and contribute to the positive social-psychological development of the individual. By helping the adolescent to develop physically and come to an increased awareness of his or her physical capabilities, the ministry to youth in wilderness trail camping can play a significant role in helping the young person build a healthy sense of identity.

SOCIAL CHARACTERISTICS AND NEEDS OF THE ADOLESCENT

The adolescent is very much aware that he or she is a social creature. Adolescents are "sometimes morbidly, often curiously, preoccupied with what they appear to be in the eyes of others as compared with what they feel they are, and with the question of how to connect the roles and skills cultivated earlier with the ideal prototypes of the day."[5] This is a threatening period in a young person's life. The changes taking place in physical, intellectual, and personality growth can be construed as a threat to one's self-image. How does the adolescent cope with radical changes in body proportions? What are the acceptable responses to the impulses that begin to infiltrate body and mind as pubescence gives way to puberty? Is there a reasonable way to cope with the many conflicting possibilities and choices presented by the immediate future?

One response is to adhere tenaciously to the social world of one's peers. The contemporary world does its share to encourage this peer culture by focusing attention upon the characteristics and needs of the adolescent. One might say that the business world, in particular, is not heisitant to exploit this particular age group. Youth form a special and profitable market with significant purchasing power. Adolescent adherence to fashions, fads, sports, and recreational activities patterned to their interests make this a lucrative market indeed.

One of the questions with which the church must deal is whether we can provide alternatives to the developing youth cultures which will offer more constructive options for the young people struggling to gain acceptance and a sense of identity in their world. I believe that the church's ministry to adolescents in wilderness trail camping takes a productive step in the right direction.

It is possible to transport some gadgetry into the wilderness, but, by and large, the nonessential cultural appendages are left at home. The supportive social structure of the peer group remains, and within that framework, in a new environment, the adolescent is challenged to new means of stimulating and enhancing his or her self-image through discovering resources within and around himself or herself. It is encouraging to note that youth are hungry for intimacy and closeness, even though the self-protective attitude they often display does not reveal this.

> Young people are tired of hearsay, tired of looking through the opaque windows of someone else's stained glass experience, tired of prepackaged answers. They want to be immediately aware, even though they are not sure of just what it is they will find. . . .
> Young people want to know themselves, nature and God, first hand, not through what they feel is their elders' distorted lenses. They want to be "in touch."[6]

The struggle to be free from the way in which other people experience the world is, in a sense, a paradox. The developing self-concept of the adolescent is heavily dependent on the way in which he or she sees other people. Much of an individual's insight comes through reflections mirrored by all the persons who have had some significant contact with him or her. "Part of his problem is to hang onto a feeling of being the same person, a person who is changing but who is still continuous and identifiable as the person he has always been and always will be."[7]

Helpful in the resolution of the problem for the adolescent is an awareness that there are societal structures which stand ready to receive him or her, regardless of the stage of life's pilgrimage in which the youth finds himself or herself. If wilderness trail camping is conducted at a level approaching its optimum potential, then it will provide a societal structure responding to the social needs of the adolescent and having a positive influence on the young person's becoming a mature person. The wilderness-experience leaders can provide the adolescent with a welcome and healthy opportunity of exploring a new identity. If the image fits into the developing self-image of the young person, then the youth will probably be eager to adopt it as part of the pattern of his or her growing social consciousness.

While some educators are reluctant to encourage the coeducational grouping of very young early adolescents, I find that coeducational camps can provide for strong same-sex relationships while at the same time providing a model for cross-sex relationships. Because of the limited size of wilderness camps (twelve persons maximum), the societal unit has a family aura without the real or imagined restrictions many adolescents identify as part and parcel of their immediate family unit. This is another positive indicator that the church's ministry in wilderness camping can provide an effective environment in which to meet the social needs of adolescents.

PSYCHOLOGICAL CHARACTERISTICS AND NEEDS OF THE ADOLESCENT

One of the major tasks of adolescence is the involvement of the individual in the establishment of an identity. This means that the young person will, of necessity, be forced to direct his or her attention inward and assess his or her own self-image. This process will include the asking of questions like "Who am I?" "What is the direction of my life?" "Am I good enough to become what I hope to be?" "How will I handle the challenges that come to me?"

Our overview of the basic physical characteristics and needs of the adolescent indicate that sound health and a satisfactory appraisal of one's physical ability and appearance contribute in a major way to the development of self-esteem. A positive self-concept gives the adolescent freedom to accept himself or herself, and this, in turn, opens the way for positive acceptance of others. This relates directly to the adolescent's self-understanding as a social creature interacting in positive and constructive ways to others.

Self-esteem, self-acceptance, and acceptance of others are all good and healthy traits, but how easily do they come to the adolescent? Is it true that the close emotional involvement of the young adolescent with family and friends, coupled with the incessant sensory stimulation of television and stereo, tend to reduce opportunities for the young person to be alone? If this is true, then the ministry to adolescents in wilderness trail camping can well be an effective means of enabling the internalization process by giving youth the opportunity to experience time alone.

A very profitable exercise in wilderness Christian education is what we call the solo experience. Older adolescents are capable of spending longer periods of time working at this than are the younger adolescents, but even short periods of time can prove helpful to the young person seeking to make the inward journey. What is involved basically is being alone, separated from the others in the group. It may be a thirty-to-sixty-minute time interval for quiet meditation, or it may be a period of from several hours to a day or more when the camper is required to fend for himself or herself, exercising basic survival skills. The benefit to the individual is obvious, even more so when the solo experience lasts for a longer period of time. The impact of the wilderness environment is most helpful in enabling one to get in touch with oneself, with God, and with the world of nature.

A sense of new and personal discovery opens up the inner world of the individual, almost demanding that the new discoveries be shared with others. I have had some of my most memorable experiences of getting in touch with young adolescents, including my own teenage children, in wilderness experiences. I have found that even very early adolescents, once they are separated from the clamor of their everyday "civilized" world, have the capability for internalization. They can get in touch with inner feelings, and they can share what is taking place with a trusted companion, regardless of age.

One of the reasons why this is possible is that the adolescent has reached a stage of intellectual development in which he or she can intellectualize about his or her own thinking. This the child cannot do. The adolescent, enjoying mobility and flexibility of thought, is able to stand off and look at himself or herself as a person.

The wilderness experience provides endless opportunities for adolescents to test their creative abilities and independent thinking. One challenge which arises frequently and demands a creative solution is crossing the wilderness stream without plunging in and getting frigidly wet in its glacier-chilled waters. The placing of stepping stones, or the cooperative hauling of small logs become methods of seeking and finding a solution to the problem. It is exciting to observe the intellectual process at work and to share in the joy of creative and successful problem solving.

The adolescent does not grow up all at once. The ability to grasp relatively complex problems mentally may be evident, while at the same time it may also be quite evident that an individual does not have the emotional sensitivity necessary to understand how one deals with the problems. This again is where the expertise of the wilderness education leader comes in. The rapidity with which the mental capabilities of the adolescent are expanding results in a great need for understanding, both from the individual involved and from others who are involved with him or her. The need to develop in emotional maturity is an important psychological need of the adolescent.

An effective key to understanding the psychological characteristics and meeting the psychological needs of adolescent youth lies in a keen sensitivity to the rapid changes, especially physical and emotional, which threaten to overwhelm the young person. In just a matter of months a boy may grow inches taller and gain fifteen to twenty pounds. A tomboyish girl suddenly becomes a young woman. Internally the physiological changes are keeping pace with the obvious outward signs of growth. Rapid growth in intellectual, emotional, and ethical maturity is also happening. Blessed is the wilderness leader who seeks to understand the resulting psychological turmoil in the life of the adolescent and who is willing to be involved in the church's ministry to these young people, seeing that their needs are met through an effective program of wilderness trail camping.

RELIGIOUS CHARACTERISTICS AND NEEDS OF THE ADOLESCENT

An awareness of the physical, social, and psychological development of the adolescent indicates that these stages of growth are also contributing to the religious and philosophical development of the young person. Concurrent with the need to understand what is happening within one's self is the adolescent's search for the meaning of life, especially in relationship to his or her own life. The early adolescent is not particularly intentional in the quest, which becomes more intensive as he or she moves into adolescence proper and late adolescence.

The early adolescent is beginning to have a sense of God which reflects a growing awareness of having to sort out the difference between what he or she has been taught and what he or she thinks. If there has been exposure to biblical knowledge, this is the time when that knowledge will be scrutinized in the light of the early adolescent's knowledge as well as his or her increasing capacity for thinking through that biblical knowledge. The early adolescent has a sense that

> . . . his thoughts of religion give him a "good feeling." He also has some idea of how God might want him to act. He thinks that prayer helps "when you're in a mess" or "at crucial times"—such times as report card time, picking a winner or loser, finding a lost ball, or falling off to sleep.[8]

The adolescent is beginning a serious quest for persons and ideas in which to have faith. He or she may begin to identify with these persons and ideas in such a way that the need for meaningful service, and the corresponding recognition of trustworthiness, will be satisfied. "At the same time, however, the adolescent fears a foolish, all too trusting commitment, and will, paradoxically, express his need for faith in loud and cynical mistrust."[9] Again, an awareness of the reasons behind the outward demonstration will be helpful to those who are seeking to minister to the adolescent.

Another factor which is helpful in understanding just where an adolescent is in the faith pilgrimage is that a youth is inclined to examine beliefs in sets. This provides an opportunity to exercise the new skill of logical thinking and to make value judgments on whether or not there are inconsistencies: inconsistencies among the beliefs and inconsistencies between the beliefs and the actions related to the beliefs. As an example, the early adolescent may formulate the following propositions out of his or her understanding of observable religious experience:

1. God loves [people].
2. The world contains many unhappy people.
3. If God loved [them], he would not make so many people unhappy.[10]

A theologian would have trouble with these propositions, but the early adolescent is not a theologian! A young person examining these statements senses their incompatability and is troubled by what he or she perceives. The propositions point up the conglomeration of ideas and beliefs which the early adolescent is trying to sort out. Unless he or she can be helped to stretch and grow in the understanding of categorical religious information and the relationship of this to perceived experience, it is entirely possible that the ultimate conclusions will be skewed, possibly leading to a denial of the hypothesis of God.

The disillusionment that overtakes many adolescents is understandable if what I have said above is true. Adolescents want to find meaning in religious faith, but if their reasoning procedure is awry, there is every reason to believe that their quest will end in failure. This failure is often expressed in cynicism and withdrawal from a relationship with the church. But even those who withdraw continue to search for some means of evaluating and assimilating the guidance data which they are receiving.

The wilderness Christian education experience can join ranks with the other approaches of the church to provide an opportunity for adolescents to stretch and grow in their quest for a meaningful religious faith. One great advantage of the wilderness camp experience is that it is removed from the stereotyped experience which physical church buildings may convey. In an out-of-doors setting, the natural openness of the adolescent heart may be more responsive to seeking and finding answers to questions about God.

We must never underestimate the value of exposing adolescents to the insightful commitment called forth by an encounter with the life of Jesus Christ as revealed in the Christian gospel. Their quest to find themselves, to discover who they are and what they should do with themselves, can be better facilitated when they have opportunities to know and work with mature Christians who demonstrate integrity of Christian faith. The mature Christian who is willing to become involved in the church's ministry to adolescents in wilderness trail camping will find many opportunities to model this integrity to those with whom they are privileged to work.

ENCOURAGING THE ADOLESCENT TOWARD BECOMING A MATURE PERSON

This brief overview of the physical, social, psychological and religious needs of the adolescent heightens the awareness that early adolescence is crucial and one of the least understood of all the stages of adolescent development. It also increases the awareness that the beginning stage of adolescence is critically important in determining the future course of the adolescent's life. This, in turn, underscores a high priority for the church to make its much-needed contribution to the guidance and development of early adolescent youth in this critical period of their lives.

The adolescent's understanding of himself or herself as a person; the still pliable image of self-concept; the perception of himself or herself as a developing social creature; the exciting stretching of mental capabilities—all of these reflect crucial stages of formation and development. The adolescent is struggling with the formation of a value system and is deeply involved in the process of developing his or her own unique personality and character. All of these processes are at work intensely throughout adolescence, and they are happening at *different* times in *different* ways to individuals who are uniquely and creatively *different*.

What is the role of the church in all this? For many adolescents, particularly those in middle or late adolescence, a revolt against "religion" (and this is essentially a revolt against religion *as they understand it*) is an integral part of adolescence. Yet, "in spite of a small minority of highly verbal cynics, religion continues to play a part in human existence and is of special value during the adolescent years in formulating ideals and standards of conduct."[11] The church's ministry to adolescents, in traditional as well as in new forms of ministry, must seek to meet each individual where he or she is, responding to the innate desire of every individual to experience a meaningful faith. The cry of the psalmist, "As a hart longs for flowing streams, so longs my soul for thee, O God. My soul thirsts for God, for the living God" (Psalm 42:1-2), is a very real cry of the adolescent heart.

The dimension of personal contact with God is what makes wilderness Christian education so thrilling and rewarding. This is not to be so presumptuous as to claim that only in the wilderness experience does this contact take place, but the added dimension of the natural environment is a positive inducement to religious experience. I shall never forget the spontaneous worship that took place the second morning of a wilderness camp experience. We had arrived at our campsite in thick fog, fog that continued through the night and into the morning hours. Suddenly, at about ten o'clock in the morning a group of early adolescents who had been sitting around listlessly and moping about the weather conditions were galvanized into action. Some were literally spinning around emitting cries of "Ooos" and "Ahs"! "Isn't God wonderful!" What had happened? The fog had begun to break and lift, and the effect was much like raising a curtain on a stage. Snow-capped peaks leaped into view; the verdant lushness of a river valley flowed away from our campsite with breathtaking beauty. Later, comments like this were noted in camper log books: "We had come up to our camp in the fog and suddenly all these different mountains were appearing. It was really neat." "The Lord cleared the sky so we could see the surroundings that He made for us to enjoy." No teacher could create such an experience, but the wilderness Christian education leader will find creative uses for such experiences when they do occur!

If we are to encourage the adolescent toward becoming a mature person, we must take advantage of the best of the traditional approaches in Christian education and be more sensitive to the values of new forms of ministry that are being developed. New ministries will have validity only as they encourage the relating of the individual to God, to self, to others, and to all of creation.

I see this coming about in a ministry to adolescents in wilderness trail camping when we provide the kinds of activities and interaction patterns that enable youth to grapple with their value schemes of acceptance, achievement, adaptability and understanding. While these schemes often clash and are many times self-defeating, it is possible to encourage growth towards wholeness, a process that accelerates as opportunities for integrity and authenticity are provided.

The next chapter will be devoted to exploring the substantive elements of wilderness learning and how these elements can best be related to the characteristics and needs of the adolescent. We will also explore the Bible as a resource for understanding the influence of wilderness experiences in bringing a nation, Israel, and various major Bible personalities to a fulfillment of their divinely ordained roles. The educational principles revealed in this study will provide further understanding for meaningful involvement with adolescents in wilderness trail camping. The conclusion of chapter 3 will look at the strengths and weaknesses of wilderness experiential education.

Chapter 3

The Wilderness Ethos and Christian Education: A Biblical Perspective

The mystique of wilderness adventuring is one that can grip the hearts of persons of all ages. Perhaps it is most exciting to youthful minds because of where they are in relation to discovering their own identity and purpose in life. From the perspective of the adolescent, the excursion into the back country may register initially as a lark, a fun thing to do. Some will view it as a time to test themselves, but the essential dynamic of what is taking place may escape them. Others are looking for a challenge, perhaps with glamorous overtones of frontier heroes who stormed the wilderness and bare-handedly wrested an existence from its sometimes hostile environment. Nevertheless, all of them will, one hopes, experience something of the spiritual values of wilderness.

ENCOUNTERING SPIRITUAL VALUES IN THE WILDERNESS EXPERIENCE

Spiritual values are basic to the wilderness ethos. Encountering them provides opportunity for personal contact with the dynamic tension of growing toward maturity. This dynamic tension recognizes the interdependent aspects of growth as well as the very necessary independent nature of the growth process. The wilderness traveler will have opportunity to discover how the wilderness can stimulate the dimension of human maturity involving understanding of, appreciation for, and assumption of responsibility. Responsibility involves living in relationship to self, others, the natural world, and most importantly God—who is the integrative center and resource for movement toward maturity.

To confront the wilderness ethos is to encounter an intangible essence that is almost impossible to put into words. What the wilderness traveler finds, however, is an experience that nourishes and sustains him or her for the rest of life. What is this wilderness ethos? What does it contribute to the individual who encounters it—the adolescent youth in particular? Is it possible that the church's ministry to adolescents through wilderness trail camping will provide at least beginning answers to these questions? Do we have enough evidence to support the contention that the physical, social, psychological and religious needs of this special age group are being met in the wilderness experience provided under the auspices of the church? Will the wilderness experience enable leaders to work with God in encouraging adolescents to move toward Christian maturity, to discover the excitement of the enabling power of God in meeting the needs of self and others, and to be good stewards of the world entrusted to their care?

The wilderness ethos includes a distinctive spirit that does not necessarily have to be interpreted in a religious vein. This distinctive spirit is one with which the secularly oriented individual can be comfortable and one which is also readily understood by persons of Christian persuasion.

> It is by contact with living nature that we are reminded of the mysterious, nonmechanical aspects of the living organism; it is by contact with nature that we begin to get, even in its lowest forms, a sense of the mystery, the independence, the unpredictableness of the living as opposed to the mechanical, and it is upon the recognition of that element in man which he shares with all living creatures that any recognition of his dignity has to be based.[1]

The Christian is convinced that the mystery of experiencing aliveness achieves its most exciting potential in knowing the Author of life. The Author of life is identified in the one who said, "I came that they may have life, and have it abundantly" (John 10:10). That conviction will be expanded continuously as persons struggle to understand, interpret, and know how God is involved in their lives, the lives of others, and the world of nature. Through this process of dynamic interaction of the individual with self, others, God, and the world of nature, the evidence of God's grace becomes visible. This is the thrust of the church's educational ministry.

In examining and applying the insights available from a serious study of the biblical approach to wilderness, we will discover principles necessary to working out answers to the questions posed above. In addition, in Bible study the following questions will be helpful: (1) Does God lead persons purposefully into wilderness experiences? If so, why? (2) Does the wilderness experience have unique values? What are they? (3) What effects do wilderness experiences have upon those who encounter them?

It is quite possible that a most important resource for knowing, understanding, and interpreting God's investment in creation has often been underrated. Can we agree with the writer who states: "For too long the church and its educational ministry has supported a strange and deafening silence. We have tried to live as if the story were unimportant"? This prominent educator would remind us that the Bible is an invaluable "textbook," for in its pages we "come to know the actor God who creates, redeems, sustains life in the past, present, and future." [2]

The value of the Bible as textbook does not lie in committing its pages to memory; its real value comes in opening new vistas into the life and soul of the people who parade across the pages of the book. When they struggle, we struggle. When they experience pain, we do, too. When they are victorious, so are we. In the biblical narrative we can be drawn into the experiences of people so intensely that we become intimately aware of the God who seeks to be in community with all people of all times—past, present and future.

The historical development of the people of the Bible is closely associated with events taking place in the natural world. It is impossible to examine the pilgrimage of the Hebrew people without becoming keenly aware that the Exodus from Egypt and the sojourn in the wilderness shaped their destiny. It is important to note that while the historical account points to the destiny-determining involvements with God in the geographical wilderness, the essence of wilderness "is not a certain locality on the map of the Middle East, but the place of God's mighty acts, significant for all believers of all times and places." [3]

God's mighty acts are not limited to geographical wilderness, whether in biblical times or in twentieth-century America. However, God's creative involvement in the essential activities—faith, love, obedience, action—of people, individuals or mass communities, is of utmost importance! This is true regardless of where the activities take place.

We have a pattern in the biblical narrative of people acting under the judgment and inspiration of God to the end that when God's will is done, a faith community becomes a reality. That same pattern is applicable to the church's educational ministry today. "If we make our life in a community of faith the context of Christian education, it will mean living each day under the judgment and inspiration of the Gospel to the end that God's community comes and God's will is done." [4]

The wilderness was the vehicle as Israel learned and grew in experience with God, the people, and the natural environment. In much the same way the wilderness today can provide the environment in which to explore and affirm the eternal principles of those relationships for modern people. The process is just as exciting for individuals. In the next section of this chapter we will explore how the wilderness learning experience was a part of the training of the children of Israel and how it influenced noted Bible personalities including Moses, Elijah, David, John the Baptist, Jesus, and Paul.

THE WILDERNESS LESSONS IN BIBLICAL PERSPECTIVE

The wilderness has been called "the womb of a fundamental datum of the religion of the Old Testament without which its development would be unintelligible."[5] Here the essential elements which contributed to Israel's life and faith are to be found.

Just the mere mention of wilderness, or desert, would immediately bring to the Jewish mind the Exodus from Egypt and the forty years spent en route. The Israelites remembered passing through a "great and terrible wilderness" (Deuteronomy 1:19), a region that was "desolate and waste" (Ezekiel 6:14), "a land of deserts and pits, . . . drought and deep darkness, . . . a land that none passes through, where no man dwells" (Jeremiah 2:6). At the same time, in spite of the desert's harsh connotations, it was also the place where God acted to deliver the people when they trusted God obediently (Exodus 15:1-18).

One of the rich experiences of wilderness travel is to awaken in the dark of the night and contemplate the majestic night splendor of the heavens. How brightly the stars shine in the blackness of the night! Similarly, the presence of God is often most keenly felt when circumstances have brought the soul to its dark and dismal night. God deliberately led Israel into the wilderness for the express purpose of bringing it to an awareness of its complete dependence upon God. This was a time for testing, a time to learn lessons of obedience (Deuteronomy 8:2).

One of the unique values of the wilderness experience for Israel was that there the people of Israel would be alone. In that aloneness with God the people would learn that the nation was chosen, not because it was bigger (Deuteronomy 7:7) or more righteous (Deuteronomy 9:4) than other nations, but because God loved Israel (Deuteronomy 7:8). The wilderness experience presented Israel with the opportunity of finding out what was really in the hearts of the people. When the nation passed the test of humility, recognizing complete and continual dependence upon God, only then were the people of Israel able to grasp the secret of God's election by which the nation would stand or fall. In order to hear the voice of God, we need our own moments of solitude. This the wilderness provides. Away from the clamor and distractions which vie for our attention, we can become aware of the still, small voice of God.

In its wilderness experience Israel faced many difficulties and miseries. The people experienced what it was like to live just a morsel away from starvation (Exodus 16:3), just a sip away from the agony of a parched throat (Exodus 15:22; 17:1-3). They learned the meaning of patience. The people learned that it was not bad to be completely dependent upon God, for God always supplied just enough for their needs. Interestingly enough, God's intervention did not change the wilderness into a paradise. The desert would not destroy Israel, yet its dangers continued to lurk at every bend in the trail. The people of Israel developed a healthy appreciation for the disciplines which wilderness living thrust upon them.

A threefold lesson came to Israel through the trials and hardships of the wilderness. The biblical narrative insisted that these lessons be learned and remembered: "The recognition of God who chose, guided and sustained his people in an act of free grace; the recognition of Israel's utter dependence upon this continued act of grace; and Israel's self-recognition in her sinfulness."[6] God used the wilderness experience to discipline and fashion Israel. The wilderness was uniquely important as God shaped and ordained this nation to be a servant people, a people surrendered to God as well as actively and uniquely involved in caring for themselves, others, and the world entrusted to their stewardship.

The influence of the wilderness upon Moses.

"From Rags to Riches" might well be the caption given to the biblical account of Moses' birth and incredible rise to status as an Egyptian prince. The story is a familiar one. In touching briefly upon some of the highlights of this man's life, our purpose is not to repeat the familiar but to acquaint ourselves with the influence of the wilderness experience upon Moses. The record of his early life indicates that he had an intense loyalty and concern for his own people. He was an individual with a keen sense of justice, fully capable of being goaded into action by a hot temper. His actions at times bordered on the reckless, carried out with courageous audacity (Exodus 2:11-15).

How did this man shift from the status of Egypt's favored son to becoming a fugitive to being remembered as the greatest of the prophets (Deuteronomy 34:10-12)? For Moses the process involved a wilderness experience. What could be interpreted as a flight for survival became a time of preparation for a monumental task.

The wilderness provided Moses with a keen awareness of God's presence. Here the most intimate confrontation of the individual with his God took place (Exodus 3:1-6; 19:3, 20; 24:12-18). It is interesting to note that closeness to God does not necessarily indicate a life that will be free of difficulty. Moses' wilderness training included lessons in patience, discipline, and humility. This was especially true in his leadership role with the people of Israel during this period. He was instructed in the necessity of being dependent upon God. He learned, sometimes with great difficulty, the importance of understanding himself—the skill of introspection. In the wilderness he experienced first-hand the frustrating disappointments of attempting to lead a "stiff necked" people. He knew the anguish of being violently angry with a people who had foolishly disobeyed God, while at the same time being willing to be removed forever from the remembrance of God if only the people could be forgiven (Exodus 32:19, 32).

The initial wilderness experience gave Moses the opportunity to be directly responsive to God's purpose for his life without major distracting influences. He was exposed to certain principles of responsible choice that were to stand him in good stead even when the going got rough. In spite of the difficulties he was privileged to bring his people to the threshold of the Promised Land. He was able to do so because he learned well the wilderness lesson of discipline. He came to a new appreciation for the wilderness itself and for its positive and negative influences upon those who ventured therein. The people, in turn, learned from him. In facing the discipline of the wilderness, which included the moral discipline of keeping God's commandments and the discipline of learning to be responsive to the holy will of God, they were finally prepared for the responsibility of entering the Promised Land.

Wilderness lessons from the life of Elijah.

Two interesting wilderness encounters were experienced by the prophet Elijah. In the first experience, Elijah was hiding in the wilderness because of his boldness in announcing the drought to King Ahab. He was also there for the express purpose of learning a lesson in faith (1 Kings 17:1-7). The wilderness was responsible for the first step in

Elijah's curriculum: "How to Have Faith in the Face of Overwhelming Odds." Elijah was secure in his hiding place as long as he had food and water. Food was no problem. As regular as clockwork, ravens brought him bread and meat, every morning and evening.

I am reminded of the time when three volunteers packed in food to one wilderness camp in the middle of our week-long stay. The youth were anticipating the arrival of the food supplies, but they had not suspected the bonus which also arrived: ice-cream bars packed in dry ice! Their exuberant joy in greeting this surprise must have somewhat resembled Elijah's appreciation of the food brought by his feathered envoys.

Water, on the other hand, was something else. With a drought in progress, Elijah watched his water supply dry up. Only the wilderness traveler knows the sinking feeling that comes when the canteen is empty and the spring is dry. God used this experience to remind Elijah that God could and would provide for the man's physical needs. Of greater importance was the lesson that God, who provides the wherewithal for daily needs, will provide the even more necessary sustenance for our involvement in the larger issues of life. In the wilderness Elijah learned to appreciate the tremendous power available when "a surrendered spirit becomes the instrument of the Infinite."[7]

The second wilderness encounter came after Elijah had found courage to confront the priests of Baal (1 Kings 18:17-46). The previous wilderness lesson prepared him for this, but Elijah was not yet ready to graduate from the wilderness school. Although God had given him a great victory, Elijah was unprepared emotionally to face the threat of losing his life at the hands of an angry Jezebel. Filled with depression and fear, he fled to the wilderness. He had not lost faith in God; he had lost faith in himself. "It is enough; now, O Lord, take away my life; for I am no better than my father" (1 Kings 19:4).

When our hearts and minds go into hiding, we become prisoners within ourselves. Add to this the cave mentality—hiding from the challenges of life surrounding us—and we are in trouble. God used the wilderness experience to bring Elijah's world view back. He regained his self-confidence. He learned the lessons of patience, discipline, humility, introspection, dependency upon God, and restoration. His blustery approach to life had brought about certain accomplishments. In the wilderness he learned that greater victories could.come about as the quiet spiritual resources made available by God were appropriated (1 Kings 19:12-18).

David, a wilderness-educated king.

David is one of the best-known and most celebrated figures in the historical narrative of Israel. We include him here for the purpose of determining how the wilderness prepared him for later responsibilities. The writer of First Samuel succinctly tells us that David was "skillful in playing (the lyre), a man of valor, a man of war, prudent in speech, and a man of good presence, and the Lord [was] with him" (1 Samuel 16:18). Even though this account may have been an embellishment by an enthusiastic admirer, David was obviously a man of many and remarkable talents.

Little is recorded of his early life except that it was a nomadic life with sheep-tending responsibilities. God is recorded as saying, "I took you from the pasture, from following the sheep, that you should be prince over my people Israel" (2 Samuel 17:7-8). The one incident of his solitary shepherd life recorded in the Scripture—his bare-handed destruction of both lions and bears in defense of his father's flocks—was a part of his plea to Saul to be allowed to confront Goliath (1 Samuel 17:34-37). His slaying of Goliath with a sling testified to skills developed while fulfilling his shepherding duties.

David appeared on the biblical scene as a youth who had everything remarkably well put together. He had a healthy self-awareness. He understood his capabilities. He was courageous and self-confident. He had a fine spiritual sensitivity. These were qualities which had apparently been worked through in many and varied wilderness experiences. David had a rich heritage; the ideas and ideals which were so much a part of his early life were retained and nurtured into maturity as he became a unique and powerful leader of his people.

If we accept the psalms which are attributed to David as truly coming out of his experiences, then we have further evidence of an individual who had learned the value of testing, patience, humility, introspection, dependence upon God, consciousness of sin, and the value of forgiveness at first hand. These were wilderness experiences which stood him in good stead when he became king. Psalm 103 further reflects the wilderness experience as it records David's sensitivity to the world of nature, from the soaring eagle to the immenseness of the heavens, to the fragility of the flower of the field. This awareness heightened David's perception of the majesty and steadfast love of the creator God.

The wilderness role in the shaping of John the Baptist.

Perhaps the most significant statement, for the purposes of this chapter, relative to the quality of individual we have in John the Baptist is that statement recorded as having been said of him by Jesus. "What did you go out into the wilderness to behold? A reed shaken by the wind?" (Luke 7:24). "A reed shaken by the wind" was a colloquialism in reference to something exceptionally common. One could find myriads of reeds wobbling in the breeze by the banks of the Jordan River. The expression could also portray an individual of fickle, vacillating character, unable to chart a stable course in any situation. But John the Baptist was not a common individual nor a man of weak convictions!

John had been foreordained to be the herald of Christ (Luke 1:13-17). He stood as the link between the old and the new covenants, announcing the coming of the Messiah. To him was given the privilege of proclaiming the "Lamb of God, who takes away the sin of the world!" (John 1:29). John introduced the one in whom the Scriptures became comprehensible and took on full significance. The task was one of great responsibility, requiring an individual who had been sharpened to keen spiritual awareness, demonstrating unique moral integrity.

When Jesus spoke concerning John, he was referring to a man of altogether extraordinary moral character. He was directing the attention of his hearers to the fact that they could look for a long time before they would be able to find a person of greater integrity or strength. John the Baptist was a prophet, "and more than a prophet" (Luke 7:26). These words suggest that "the Lord himself regarded John as an eschatological symbol and event, a fulfillment as well as a bearer of prophecy, a portent as well as a herald of the kingdom of God."[8]

Because of the significance of wilderness in the history of the people, "it was not by chance that, in order to prepare the people for the eschatological advent of the Lord, it was precisely in the desert that John the Baptist's ministry was located."[9] Set free from the political machinations inherent in the settled communities, the people, through John, were able to become more alert spiritually. The threefold lesson of the wilderness was grasped, not only by John, but by those who came to hear him: God is the initiator of all; we are dependent upon his grace; self-awareness and consciousness of sin are realities we must confront. The outcome of their coming to grips with the threefold lesson was the realization of the apocalyptic hope—restoration of fellowship with God.

Christ in the wilderness: its impact upon his ministry.

In the introduction of his Gospel, Mark noted the close association of Jesus to John the Baptizer as Jesus' ministry began. Of special interest is the fact that the locality was the wilderness. Jesus came from Nazareth to be baptized by John and following that significant event, immediately entered into the temptation experience. Commentators are generally agreed that these important incidents in the life of Jesus did indeed take place in the wilderness.

The significance of this is the understanding of Jesus as more than an isolated individual concerned only for his own righteousness; he was a "member of a body of people whose heritage and predicament he [shared] and, like Moses he [did] not divorce himself from the sins of his people, but [was] bound up with them." [10] In this identity he demonstrated his humility, participating with others in following John's call to the wilderness to receive the baptism of repentance (Philippians 2:6-7). Israel was designated to be God's chosen, or son, in the wilderness (Exodus 4:11; Hosea 11:1); Jesus fulfilled the ideal sonship as a representative of the people in his baptism in the wilderness (Mark 1:11). In undergoing baptism in the wilderness Jesus underscored his understanding of what the Exodus into the wilderness meant: "Only Jesus fully realized what it meant to go out into the wilderness: it meant the determination to live under the judgment of God." [11]

The temptation narrative picks up this theme. In an environment completely free from the pressures of family life and society, Jesus could wrestle with the major issues of life. We cannot begin to identify with the magnitude of the temptation struggle. The cosmic scope of what Jesus experienced goes far beyond our finite personal encounters with the meaning of life, including sin. We can, however, experience Christ's victory as we appropriate the lessons of his wilderness encounter for our own lives.

In the silence and solitude of the wilderness, Jesus sought to determine exactly what God's will for him involved. The process of learning how to face difficult decisions and to differentiate between the plausible voice of false alternatives and God's voice of truth was a part of the testing out there. Regardless of what interpretations we place upon the individual, social, and spiritual lessons of the temptations, the basic lessons are the same. Jesus found reaffirmation for his understanding and commitment to discipline, humility, patience and absolute dependance upon God. The battle would go on but the victory had been established. Throughout his earthly life the wilderness remained the place where he could go for times of renewal and reaffirmation. Here Jesus found illustrations to make his witness powerfully pertinent.

Above all, he found spiritual strength that could never be taken by surprise or shaken.

Paul's Arabian experience.

The biblical record of Paul's Arabian experience is scanty. After his dramatic conversion experience on the Damascus road, he simply states, "I did not confer with flesh and blood, nor did I go up to Jerusalem to those who were apostles before me, but I went away into Arabia, and again I returned to Damascus" (Galatians 1:16-17). We are not certain where his Arabian experience took place. Some would like to believe that he retreated to the Sinai region, an intriguing suggestion in the light of both Moses' and Elijah's wilderness experiences. What we can be certain of is Paul's expressed need to have a period of time to free himself from human persuasions, including those of his contemporaries already serving as apostles.

> . . . Obviously there is in the desert an awayness, an apartness rarely equaled anywhere else. There social influences are reduced to a minimum; there it is easier to cultivate the vertical awareness of God without hinderance from the horizontal affairs of men. A gospel which had come to Paul directly from God could be pondered and spelled out in the eternal silence of God.[12]

Paul had gone through a dramatically soul-shattering experience. The murderous momentum of his life had come to an unbelievably abrupt halt. His intellectual blueprints were being revamped drastically and he needed time to piece together the new design according to Christ's larger terms and patterns. He needed to learn to march to the beat of a different drummer. The intent of the wilderness experience was not to destroy the driving forces within Paul but to redirect them. And, much as one does not shift from high to reverse at ninety-five miles an hour, so this man needed to shift into "neutral" to get in touch with God. He needed time to grow in his newfound fellowship with Christ so that he could return to his society in full possession of himself and, at the same time, totally controlled by the gospel he would proclaim.

The wilderness lessons which had made their mark upon other great personages of the Bible found an apt student in Paul. Words like patience, self-control, humility, and gentleness became the backbone of his message to the early church. A mind that had already been sharpened by intellectual study now came to grips with practical experiences which left their indelible impression that God is the initiator of all, all persons are dependent upon God's grace, and by the Holy

Spirit self-awareness and consciousness of sin are realized.

Paul's intellectual awareness of his nation's historical background, coupled with his newfound experience in Christ, issued forth in a dramatic presentation of the Christian sacraments as analogous to Israel's wilderness journey. The analogy was undoubtedly sharpened by his own Arabian experience. (See 1 Corinthians 10:2, Romans 6:3, Galatians 3:27, 1 Corinthians 10:3-4.)

The Apostle's understanding of wilderness, coupled with his own wilderness experience, became the catalyst for his message of God's grace. Experiencing God's unmerited favor freed Paul from bondage, but this newfound freedom did not grant him license for spiritual pride or freedom to flaunt his new state of spirituality. The effectiveness of Paul's witness, in life as well as word, is ample evidence of the positive influence of his wilderness sojourn.

ETHOS, EDUCATION, AND EXPERIENCE: A SUMMARY STATEMENT

In this chapter I have endeavored to point up the essential or constituent elements of the wilderness learning experience. While at some points the wilderness ethos is somewhat ethereal, at other points it is remarkably substantial. From our biblical perspective we have encountered experiences verifying that these divergent, yet complementary, elements are present in the wilderness experiences.

In our ministry to adolescents we are endeavoring to encourage the young person towards becoming a mature person. From our study in chapter two we saw that the challenge is not one to be taken lightly. The physical, social, psychological, and religious needs of this age group demand the best efforts that those who seek to minister to them can put forth. If a specific type of ministry can complement the efforts already being made in our Christian education system, then we have a responsibility to utilize that ministry.

The insights from our research into the biblical perspective of the contribution of wilderness experiences affirms our responsibility to make use of those insights in ministering to the adolescent. Awareness of the values of wilderness learning reinforces its value in the educational process. We must remember that wilderness lessons were not grasped by the biblical characters in exactly the same manner nor were the lessons encountered in similar situations and circumstances. The biblical personages were unique, as are adolescents. Individual needs vary, and the insights experienced must fit the situation. Yet, inherent in the experiences is a unifying thread of influence seeking to move individuals through healthy growth toward maturity. This maturity includes a better understanding of and appreciation for self, others, God, and the world in which we live.

The uniqueness of the wilderness education experience is that the environment provides for helping "persons regain their God-given ability to wonder and create; to dream and fantasize, imagine and envision. . . ."[13] The real genius of wilderness education lies in acting and reflecting upon its ethos, grappling with the lessons that can come alive with the assistance of a biblical perspective, and appreciating the results in accordance with individual needs. As we seek to live individually and corporately under the judgment and inspiration of biblical truth, as we learn to live independently and interdependently with ourselves, others, the world of nature, and God, the door is open for God's will to be done and his kingdom to come into the midst of our lives.

The positive effects of experiential education.

The student who is directly involved in working out the relationship of the gospel to his or her life situation has a distinct advantage over the student who is attempting to apply the gospel to life in a hypothetical situation.

An interesting illustration of this principle of learning is given by Marshall McLuhan.

> He points out that if a five-year old is moved to a foreign country, and allowed to play freely for hours with his new companions, with no language instruction at all, he will learn the new language in a few months, and will acquire the proper accent too. He is learning in a way which has significance and meaning for him, and such learning proceeds at an exceedingly rapid rate. But let someone try to *instruct* him in a new language, basing the instruction on the elements which have meaning for the *teacher*, and learning is tremendously slowed, or even stopped.[14]

I had a similar experience to that related by McLuhan when I was six years old. I moved to Denmark where I was allowed to learn the language by the method cited. I had no formal language instruction; I am unable to read or write Danish today. But I am able to carry on conversations with native Danes when the opportunity arises! Although almost five decades have elapsed, my Danish friends compliment me on my correct accent.

The point of this is that it graphically illustrates the important elements of experiential learning. One of the significant elements is the quality of personal involvement. When a person is feelingly and cognitively immersed *in* the learning event, he or she can become totally involved. A trail leader can explain and demonstrate the difference between a square knot and a granny knot to a camper without much apparent success. However, when a camper has trouble untying a stuff sack, when it's time to get out the sleeping bag, a stubborn granny knot can inspire the camper to learn to tie a square knot very quickly!

Experiential learning has a pervasive quality. Behavior, attitude, even the learner's personality, may reflect the significance of the growth that is taking place. The basic accomplishment of getting to the end of a grueling uphill hike may elicit an exuberant proclamation—"I did it!"—with observable positive effects on behavior, attitude, and personality. The learner is the one who does the most important evaluating of experiential learning. If a need is being met, he or she is the first to know. If the experience has contributed to what he or she wants to know, the individual will be the first to sense this. The essence of experiential learning is meaning. "When such learning takes place, the element of meaning to the learner is built into the whole experience." [15]

The environment, including church school, site camp, and wilderness, has an important impact upon the learner. It "contains objects, people, events, and human situations that stimulate and provoke a person's internal capacities." [16] The learner is focused upon as the one who discovers and applies spiritual meanings. The more nearly the environment becomes a part of a natural experience (not contrived or staged), the more quickly learning may take place.

There are educators who would argue that since the activity method seems most responsible for the effectiveness of outdoor education, why not bring more activity/experience-oriented learning into the formal classroom? Would not this satisfactorily accomplish what we hope to do in the out-of-doors? The answer is simply that some experiences cannot be duplicated in the classroom. I know of no way, for instance, of duplicating the experience we had one August afternoon on the crest trail. We were caught on the trail in a sudden rainstorm complete with lightning. While trying to be aware of necessary safety measures—stay off high ridges, avoid taking shelter under a tall tree—we observed a lightning strike on an adjoining ridge. We could soon see the fire burning in a somewhat isolated clump of trees. Within the hour a forest service aircraft was over the scene to observe the potential fire danger. The aircraft left, only to return shortly, dropping two smoke-jumpers in the vicinity of the blaze. As we watched this drama unfold, the storm passed on, the fire was controlled, and a beautiful rainbow provided the backdrop for our campsite. Try to duplicate that in the classroom!

Our devotional study for that day was based on Deuteronomy 4:32-35 which reviews how God had provided for the people in their wilderness experience. We had talked about how Israel arrived safely in the Promised Land only because God met them and guided them through every situation they encountered. Our experience that afternoon really made our awareness of God's self-disclosure in nature come alive! We had a new appreciation for human involvement in caring for our natural resources, and the rainbow reminded us of how the Spirit of God indwells every relationship. It matters not whether the concern is for personal/group safety or for preservation of natural resources. God enables all persons to fulfill their common discipleship and to abide in Christian hope.

The weaknesses of wilderness experiential education.

One of the first weaknesses to surface in wilderness experiential education, especially for the ministry of the Christian church, is the lack of available materials. This lack is also an advantage, but in the advantage lies a hidden danger. When materials are not available, churches and leaders involved in wilderness camping are stimulated to develop their own programs. However, if the intensity of research and preparation is haphazard or shallow, the final result will not measure up to the Christian education objective.

Another readily observed weakness is the difficulty of finding and recruiting adequate leadership. In addition, participation in a wilderness experience is costly. Proper equipment is a must, and that equipment can be quite expensive. Timing may be a problem when capable persons are prevented from participating because of scheduling conflicts.

In combating weaknesses, experiential education—religious or secular—must be developed in accordance with high-level educational standards, aims, and methods. "The greatest danger that attends its future is . . . the idea that it is an easy way to follow, so easy that its course may be improvised, if not in an impromptu fashion, at least almost from day to day or from week to week."[17] If we are not willing to spend the time necessary to develop adequate leadership, programming, and curriculum, then we would be wise to stay out of the wilderness education field.

Excellent programming ideas and curriculum materials are being developed. Educational researchers are continually at work seeking to improve the old as well as to provide new methodology for our ministries in church schools and site camps. We dare not do less in making the most of the opportunities available to us in bringing to maturity the church's ministry to adolescents in wilderness trail camping!

Part II.

The Practice of Wilderness Christian Education

The questions asked by participants in wilderness camping seminars are usually concerned with the responsibilities of leaders; the amount and kinds of experience required; the role of the leader as teacher; and the best methods of preparing intellectually, spiritually, and physically for the camping experience. Prospective leaders are interested in group-leadership skills. Values clarification is a tool used increasingly by educators. Will values clarification exercises assist the leader in enabling campers to understand themselves better and to stretch and grow? What other tools are available to assist in the process of experiential education?

What about the actual event? If I have never participated in a trail camp, what do I do? How much do I need to know about equipment? Food? Clothing? Are there survival skills with which I need to be familiar? What about camp and trail safety? Should someone be skilled in first aid? Is it necessary for the well-being of the group to establish ground rules for the anticipated program? What are the correct procedures in the event of an accident?

Where can I find the resources that must be available for planning and conducting a wilderness camp experience? Is there a need for follow-up after the camp has concluded? How do I go about putting together a trail annual? Is there value in holding a reunion of the trail-camp group? When?

If these are the kinds of questions you are asking, please read on. Out of my experiences I share answers to these and other questions, which I have found to be helpful. I hope that you will find many practical ideas to help you enjoy the tremendous rewards that come through youth ministry in a wilderness setting.

Chapter 4

The Wilderness Leader

The key to effective wilderness education will be found in the quality of leadership. Trail leaders and counselors alike must be adequately oriented and educated to the wilderness philosophy and to the derivative purposes of wilderness camping as they complement the purposes of the church. This requires a good grasp of the philosophy and the purposes of the wilderness experience by the persons involved. A workable understanding of the objectives and goals of wilderness Christian education is essential, and a high level of individual commitment in one's personal faith is extremely important. The leader who has not grappled seriously with the meaning of living out his or her commitment to Jesus Christ in daily life is ill-prepared to help youth encounter the process of developing a Christian life-style for themselves. You cannot share what you do not have any more than you can come back from a place you have not been!

Daily experiences on the wilderness trail are chock-full of opportunities for our faith to be shared as we become involved in encouraging and nurturing the faith of our campers. As leaders, we, too, may experience testing, and we may have many opportunities to encourage campers whose faith is tested.

On the fourth day of one trail camp we had hiked to a lookout on a high ridge for the express purpose of enjoying the view. We had been told that it was possible to see for miles—spectacular scenery that included majestic peaks, verdant river valleys, and ridges undulating to the horizon. What did we see? Fog! Fog so thick that at times we lost sight of one another on the trail. Some of the campers began to grumble. "If God made all this beauty up here, why doesn't he let us enjoy it?" One of the counselors called attention to the intricacies of creation that were right under foot. "If we had that fantastic view we came up here to see, we would miss out on the other things that are all around us—like the tiny flowers with dew drops on them." Later in our reflection time the comment was made, "That's how we are in our spiritual lives sometimes. We focus our eyes on the great things ahead of us and we forget to live and experience the small and beautiful things that are all around us." Here indeed is a valuable spiritual lesson that shares more easily when we make it a practical part of our everyday living. A capable leader will open windows enabling campers to catch a fresh glimpse of how they can best cope with life situations.

The leader of youth must be an individual who is in touch with a holistic concept of understanding himself or herself. The leader-type person will demonstrate that he or she is in touch with "both his outer way of sharing in his physical and social world and his inner conduct toward himself."[1] Being in touch with one's inner self includes sensitivity to intellectual, emotional, and integrative spiritual values. The leader must seek to understand and to develop a sensitivity to the variety of forces that surround him or her as well as those that are a part of his or her internal vitality. The presence of Christ, given freedom to control our lives, will go a long way toward bringing this about!

The degree to which the leader is able to demonstrate such awareness and faith will soon become apparent on the trail. The veneer that stands up fairly well in the "thermostatically controlled" environment of our city surroundings quickly begins to crack and peel in the harsh "climate" of the wilderness! Physical fatigue, freezing rain (trying its best to drown out breakfast preparations), the kettle of hot cocoa kicked over by a careless camper—all serve to hone tempers razor sharp. The preparation for successful living in the wilderness begins before one reaches the trail head.

IMPORTANT FACTORS IN LEADERSHIP QUALIFICATIONS

All of us learn from experience. The pressures of life too often push us from one experience to another without adequate time for reflection, learning, or appreciation. The wilderness experience provides time for each individual to make the effort to reflect on what is taking place. Trained leadership can encourage the asking of such questions as "Can I identify specifically and concretely what happened in this experience? . . . Who was responsible and who was irresponsible? Were results satisfying or disappointing?"[2] These questions will make the most sense when the wilderness leader has learned to slow his or her life down to

the point where he or she can ask them meaningfully, in a personal
way.

When looking at questions like "Who was responsible, and who was
irresponsible?" "Were results satisfying or disappointing?" it is important to avoid the trap of blaming someone in the event the experience
has had a negative effect. There may have been valuable catharsis in
biblical times in having a "scapegoat" to send off into the wilderness,
but we hope that present-day wilderness trail leaders will have developed
skills in avoiding scapegoating.

Our final meal on one camp—we elected as a group to have stew—
was a horrendous experience! It would be impossible to describe how
utterly bad the stew tasted. What had happened? A camper, hastily
stuffing his backpack, had put a loosely capped fuel container in the
same compartment with the food package! As the meal was prepared
the contaminated package was added, unnoticed, and the new flavor
was only noticeable when our taste buds encountered the stew. Wow!
Fortunately, no one became ill. It would have been easy to "tar and
feather" the culprit, but our week's experience together had brought
us to the place where we could discuss what had happened and make
a real learning experience out of it. Each of those campers will probably
remember that a fuel bottle is always tightly capped and placed in a
separate pocket in the pack so it will stay in an upright position!

A look at the Outward Bound leadership model.

Leaders will find it helpful to try to anticipate, to "picture," the
process which will help them to participate effectively in the wilderness
education experience. The first of two illustrations (see p. 78) sche-
matically presents the process used in the Outward Bound schools.[3] As
indicated, the leader, or instructor, has a very important role to play
in all that takes place. That person must be the enabler, facilitator,
interpreter, encourager, model—to the end that the camper, or learner,
has been effectively oriented to the process of living and learning. The
diagram is self-explanatory and has much to offer any wilderness leader
who will study it and attempt to put its principles into practice.

Perhaps the following experience will illustrate the major points of
that process. Four of us, myself as trail leader accompanied by three
counselors, had gone on an overnight to finalize our plans for an
upcoming trail camp. Though it was very late spring, we encountered
more snow on the ground than we had anticipated. Because of the late
melt, rivers were running quite high. To reach our projected campsite

THE OUTWARD BOUND PROCESS

Instructor intervenes throughout process as a Translator; Initiator; Trainer; Maintainor; Authority Figure; Exemplar; . . .

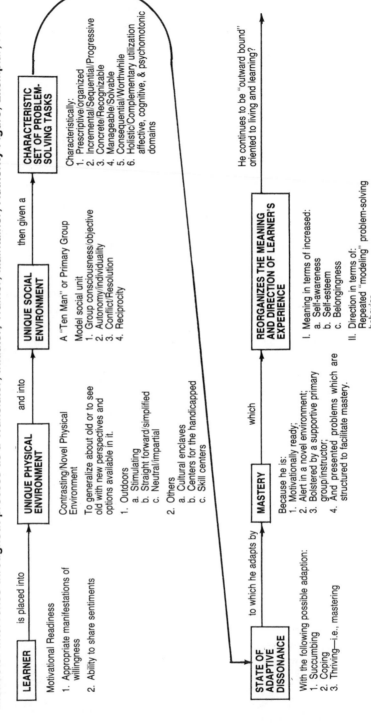

LEARNER is placed into

Motivational Readiness

1. Appropriate manifestations of willingness
2. Ability to share sentiments

and into **UNIQUE PHYSICAL ENVIRONMENT**

Contrasting/Novel Physical Environment

To generalize about old or to see old with new perspectives and options available in it.

1. Outdoors
   a. Stimulating
   b. Straight forward/simplified
   c. Neutral/impartial

2. Others
   a. Cultural enclaves
   b. Centers for the handicapped
   c. Skill centers

and into **UNIQUE SOCIAL ENVIRONMENT**

A "Ten Man" or Primary Group

Model social unit
1. Group consciousness/objective
2. Autonomy/individuality
3. Conflict/Resolution
4. Reciprocity

then given a **CHARACTERISTIC SET OF PROBLEM-SOLVING TASKS**

Characteristically:
1. Prescriptive/organized
2. Incremental/Sequential/Progressive
3. Concrete/Recognizable
4. Manageable/Solvable
5. Consequential/Worthwhile
6. Holistic/Complementary utilization affective, cognitive, & psychomotonic domains

He continues to be "outward bound" oriented to living and learning?

STATE OF ADAPTIVE DISSONANCE

With the following possible adaption:
1. Succumbing
2. Coping
3. Thriving—i.e., mastering

to which he adapts by **MASTERY**

Because he is:
1. Motivationally ready;
2. Alert in a novel environment;
3. Bolstered by a supportive primary group/instructor;
4. And presented problems which are structured to facilitate mastery.

which **REORGANIZES THE MEANING AND DIRECTION OF LEARNER'S EXPERIENCE**

I. Meaning in terms of increased:
   a. Self-awareness
   b. Self-esteem
   c. Belongingness

II. Direction in terms of:
   Repeated "modeling" problem-solving behavior

for the night we had to cross a river on a foot log, normally not an unpleasant experience. However, with the high water now raging beneath the log it became a spine-tingling adventure! We were learners, in a unique physical environment as well as a unique social environment, and we had a problem-solving task ahead of us.

As leader I felt that I must not reveal the fact that to me the log across the river looked like a half-inch tightrope stretched across Niagara Falls! It would have been easy to abort our plans and find another place to camp. Common sense told me that the crossing was not too difficult to accomplish (a couple with a small child passed our campsite later), so I carefully—prayerfully—made my way across. All of us mastered the "state of adaptive dissonance" (see chart on p. 78) and came to a new sense of self-awareness and self-esteem. In a postcamp evaluation the one woman counselor wrote, "The pretrip hike was really necessary for me. Going across logs over a river without six kids watching gave me the confidence I needed since that was the one thing about which I was apprehensive. When I saw I could do it, it really took away the major part of my anxieties about the trip. I must add that I felt every crossing on the hike was a snap compared to the one we did on the prehike!"

Church wilderness education programs can learn much from the Outward Bound methodology. Indeed, it has been said that "OUTWARD BOUND has become one of the leading exponents of adventure-based education in America. . . . The term OUTWARD BOUND has become synonymous with adventure education."[4]

An alternate approach to the relationship of leader and experience.

The second diagram by John and Lela Hendrix (see p. 80) takes a somewhat different approach, but many of the same principles are involved.[5] The process begins when leaders and campers make the commitment to invest their energies and abilities in the wilderness experience. *Buying in and owning the process* can begin when the group is introduced. It is a process that begins in the leaders long before the event takes place. Leaders cannot come to the first day of a trail camp without prior preparation. This would invite disorganization, if not disaster!

The strategy I follow is first of all to involve the campers in the process of determining who will be in which small group. With a maximum of twelve persons in a wilderness trail camp, the total mem-

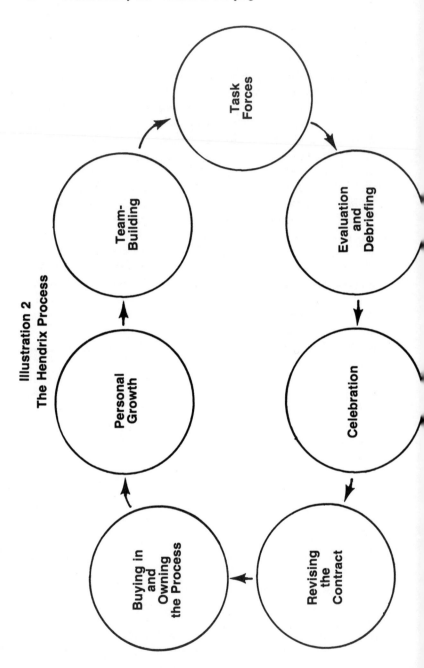

Illustration 2
The Hendrix Process

bership in itself constitutes a small group. However, small groups of three to five persons within the overall grouping contribute significantly to the experiential education process. Campers are free to choose with whom they would like to participate rather than being assigned to a group. Some of the activities suggested in chapter 5 may be helpful in enabling individuals to become acquainted. If the camper has no preference, or would rather be assigned to a group, that is done. Choice of tent partners is also by preference, the only restriction being that in coeducational camps the tenting arrangement is by same sex. In my experience with junior high and middle high camps, the youth are adamant about being in same-sex groups, but they enjoy the congeniality of the overall mixed groups.

Food distribution becomes the next natural group process, and the knowledge that everyone is taking on more weight to carry begins a keen awareness of what the other person is doing—if only to insure that the distribution is equitable! I have been impressed by the obvious consideration of the youth when there happens to be a physically undersized person in the group. That awareness is part of the personal growth principle.

The leadership process in encouraging personal growth.

Personal growth can occur as the individual is helped to identify where he or she is in the growth process. The wilderness experience will assist in developing this identity and in building confidence along with growth. Two of the younger girls on one trail camp were determined not to let the words of caution about the muddiness of the trail hinder their newfound freedom in the wilderness. They discovered the hard way that six-inch boots in eight inches of mud creates an immediate problem! As we approached our first campsite they were wet, cold, and very negative about the whole experience. They were willing to talk about it, though, and after getting cleaned up and starting the process of drying out their boots, had a better understanding of the value of trail rules and counselor concern. Subsequent actions during the week testified to the fact that personal growth had taken place.

Household tasks as a valuable leadership resource in team building.

Team building will occur when each participant is helped to discover the unique and indispensable part that each plays in accomplishing a common task. One of the first times a camper becomes somewhat aware of this is at mealtime. The effort of putting a meal together lends itself perfectly to an educational experience in team building. One person will have to get water; another will check the stove to be sure that it is ready for use and will light it at the appropriate time. Others will busy themselves with the actual preparation of the meal. We had a near disaster as one camper mixed the graham cracker crust in with the blue berries because he misread the directions for the blueberry cobbler. What an awful looking mess! I appreciated his prayer later when he said "Thanks, Lord, for making this taste good even though I messed it all up." It is apparent that the principles of "buying in and owning the process" and "personal growth" are an integral part of the learning cycle.

A look at the remaining principles of the Hendrix leadership process.

Developing the daily strategy, evaluating goals and objectives, determining a "game plan" for the day, become *task force* responsibilities. What do we do about the intended day hike to a high mountain lake when fog has reduced visibility to zero? At given times in the overall experience, as well as at the conclusion, it will be necessary to take time for *evaluation and debriefing*. This is the time to allow expressions of feeling about any part of the process, and to suggest specific ways to improve. This is an important step in learning to plan and planning to learn!

Celebration is a very important part of this leadership model. There are times when it can be planned, but more often than not it will be spontaneous. It may come on a high mountain ridge overlooking a breathtaking wilderness vista, or it may occur as the group closes out the day around the campfire (when ecologically possible and permitted). Celebration grows out of the encounters—people to people, people to nature, people to God—and the variety of experiences shared.

> Last night around the campfire we shared our experiences of the week. It turned out that everyone had as good a time as I did. That makes me happy to know that everyone, not just a few, had a blast. I'm gonna miss all those times of uncontrollable laughter, rolling over logs, murdering muscles on switchbacks, yodeling, and imitating fog horns, etc., etc., etc.

Revising the contract brings the group to that place where the process begins all over again. It may involve a disruption of the agenda; it may come about by anticipating a new or different set of circumstances influencing the "game plan." Additional or new data impinging upon an activity may force a renegotiation of the activity or program. The key again lies in how well the leadership can enable the process. The Outward Bound process is directional; the Hendrix process is cyclical. Both of them have common elements and both have valuable contributions to make to leaders of wilderness education experiences.

Putting together our personal leadership style.

Many of us will have to struggle to break free from the binding influences of the "schooling-instructional paradigm."[6] Church schools have accepted the public school as a model of education and have built their instructional format around the patterns of secular pedagogy and psychology. "Education grounded in Christian faith cannot be a vehicle for control; it must encourage an equal sharing of life in community, a cooperative opportunity for reflection on the meaning and significance of life."[7] This principle, applied to wilderness Christian education, could well make the wilderness camping experience the most exciting option for the church's education program today. It certainly presents a challenge to the wilderness leader.

Almost unlimited possibilities face the trail leader in meeting the challenge of wilderness Christian education. The possibilities are there because of the way the wilderness experience enables campers to have maximum exposure to direct purposeful involvements in an intimate small group setting. The leader who sees these possibilities can develop a leadership style aimed at utilizing these experiences effectively.

GROWTH EXPERIENCES ANTICIPATED BY LEADERS

Let us look briefly at the kinds of growth experiences that the wilderness trail leader anticipates may take place within the camper.

Self-awareness.

First of all, youth (leaders, too!) will come to a heightened self-awareness involving a more accurate understanding of personal physical capabilities or limitations. Our trail camps are generally planned to include at least one hard day's hike. This will usually include a rather generous elevation gain. In his evaluation one counselor wrote: "I think planning at least one hard day's hike is a good idea. It can help campers gain confidence in themselves as they accomplish a physical task they felt incapable of doing." I would add that it is not just the youth who have second thoughts about their abilities to stick with it on a tough hiking day!

This same counselor succinctly focused on the importance of realizing capabilities *and* limitations of the individual members of the trail group. "Since the campers all have different capabilities and limitations, the leaders would need to be very aware of these. The biggest problem to overcome would be to get the campers to focus on the idea of discovering their own potentials and limits and avoid making comparisons with their peers."

A heightened self-awareness of personal physical capabilities or limitations will include an increased awareness of one's responses under stress and, we hope, better self-control. It will also bring about sharpening of mental awareness through encouraging the thinking/reflecting process. An increased self-awareness leads the camper to a greater understanding of his or her interdependency with all that is to be experienced.

As a leader I have encountered young people who have a much greater capacity than I for pushing up a grade. I recall the time that a group of us were struggling up a series of switchbacks with fairly full packs. I was in the lead and becoming more and more frustrated as the campers behind me were almost walking up my back. It was only after we had reached the top—in a state of near exhaustion—that I discovered something which in retrospect seems almost funny. While I had been pushing to stay ahead of the campers, they had been pushing to keep up with me! As we talked this over, I realized that my irritation with being followed so closely was due to my lack of understanding of what was going on. Thinking and reflecting with the campers about what had happened helped us all to come to a better understanding of the physical, social, and mental factors involved in the experience. We all came to a better understanding of our interrelatedness with each other and our interdependency with the factors influencing that situation: trail conditions, people, and inner attitudes.

Self-confidence.

The wilderness leader will anticipate a second area of growth: the camper will develop greater self-confidence. This may come about through physical effort requiring endurance and stamina, the kind necessary to move a thirty-five- to forty-five-pound pack five miles up a trail rising 3,000 feet in elevation.

Increased self-confidence will also come about through social encounter as one learns to assess personal strengths and weaknesses and to accept the critical and creative assessment of others. We have a standing rule in our camps that everyone is responsible for practicing good ecological manners. Leaders set the example from the very beginning of the camp. For some campers, following the rule may mean the breaking of bad habits. Carelessly tossing even the smallest bit of litter on the trail carries a big message to the other campers. Practicing good habits builds self-confidence and reflects a valid behavior pattern practiced by the leaders. Campers can be challenged to emulate good wilderness manners and, in the process, will begin to develop initiative in controlling their own actions and in encouraging similar actions in others.

Just as developing and exercising initiative contributes to building self-confidence, so will discovering the benefits of self-motivation. This becomes evident as campers develop skill in the basic routines of selecting a campsite, setting up tents, breaking camp, unpacking and repacking backpacks. A sloppily packed, unbalanced pack is usually not in evidence after the second day of camp. A neatly packed pack with weight properly distributed is much easier to carry. Pride in the way a tent has been erected and in a well-policed campsite reflects increased self-motivation and growing self-confidence. The wilderness leader may anticipate the growth of self-confidence as opportunities are given to the camper to check out his or her actions with self/counselor/peer evaluation.

Spiritual self-identity.

Third, wilderness Christian education provides experiences which may lead to a growing spiritual self-identity. This can come by gaining and sharing insights into practical biblical truths. I have observed this taking place as young people talk together around the campfire with a freedom that has come out of the intense, sustained, and close group experiences of the day. I can visualize the disciples of Jesus doing the very same thing! A growing spiritual self-identity develops as the camper becomes more aware of what it means to be created in the image of God—"I am an integral part of creation yet uniquely distinctive"; then, as the camper realizes his or her personal worth—"I am important in God's sight." Again, as the youth gains a deepening insight and appreciation of interdependence with all that is, spiritual self-identity is more clearly brought into focus. The alert wilderness leader will encourage youth to make a personal commitment to Jesus

Christ as Savior and Lord if the camper has not already done so.

A heightened sense of appreciation.

Finally, the trail leader anticipates that the camper will have a new appreciation of *self* through testing of new skills and recognition of inner strengths; of *others* through exercising and accepting leadership and followership roles (discovering the ramification of the servant role); of the *environment* through an awareness of the principles of ecology and the fundamentals of survival; and of *God* through fresh personal encounters with God's creation and God's creatures, including oneself.

As leaders, we can discover no better example than Jesus as one who made the most of direct, purposeful experiences. The immediate environment, including people, objects, and the world of nature, was made a part of the impact of learning. "He used everything around him to teach—the place, the time of day, the people, the children, the clothing, the soil, the trees, the lunch of a boy, grains of wheat, and a Roman coin. With these things he shaped a learning situation."[8] We would do well to emulate our Lord. I believe that good wilderness teachers may become better classroom teachers as a result of a wilderness education experience.

SELECTING AND TRAINING LEADERS

We need to be sensitive to the natural qualifications and capabilities of wilderness camp leaders. These qualifications and capabilities should be undergirded by a mature yet growing understanding of what it means to be committed personally to Jesus Christ as Savior and Lord. The gifted leader is one who looks for ways to sharpen the intuitive and acquired abilities which he or she possesses, while continuing to grow. Stretching toward what he or she might ultimately become is an active, ongoing process with its optimum potential in the leader who is seeking to grow in Christ through worshiping God and serving fellow human beings.

Leaders directing a wilderness camp have two initial responsibilities. The first is careful selection of capable persons to serve on the camp staff; the second is to see that these persons are trained.

> It is important that the director be familiar with all the leadership training opportunities available and use those which will be the most effective in his particular situation. . . . A reading program should be suggested by the director. The guidance materials basic to the camp program should be distributed early. If it is possible for the staff to meet frequently during

the winter and spring, discussions may be held based on certain chapters designated by the director. He will want to recommend several books that will be helpful.[9]

See the bibliography in this book for suggestions of many helpful resource books.

Preparing for the wilderness camp experience.

Wilderness trail camp leaders will find it extremely helpful to take time for an overnight outing prior to the camp itself. This might well take place on a portion of the trail which will be used for the wilderness experience, and thus provide a "shakedown" for the staff. Familiarizing themselves with the operation of equipment, testing their own physical readiness for the trip, and talking through their plans to achieve educational goals can be done effectively in this setting. This is an excellent time for staff to review goals they have established in accordance with their camp purpose as derived from their philosophy of wilderness camping. It is a time to strive for increased openness and objectivity among members of the wilderness-experience team. Values-clarification skills, community-building exercises, and communication skills can be practiced (see chapter 5). The staff should be thoroughly familiar with the devotional guide, taking time on this outing to test some of the spiritual lessons it suggests.

The wilderness leader will keep up-to-date on all the legal requirements and regulations affecting the wilderness camping experience. This means keeping in touch with the supervisory governmental agencies responsible for regulating the size of groups permissible in a given area (twelve is the maximum group size currently permitted in a designated wilderness area). Agencies which issue the necessary permits for wilderness travel must be contacted. Permits can be obtained from the district ranger station or applied for by mail. When applying by mail, allow at least ten days for the permit to come to you. Be knowledgeable of regulations established by agencies which indicate areas closed to camping, density of campers permitted at given sites, campfire regulations, and setbacks from lakes and streams, to name a few. Government regulations that affect camping are becoming more numerous, but they *must* be observed. Although wilderness rangers are few and far between, they have been known to scratch on the flap of your tent, asking to see your wilderness permit! The forest service information telephone number is listed in the white pages under "United States Government, Agriculture Department of."

The importance of physical fitness.

Not everyone will be physically able to become a wilderness camp leader. Surprisingly, however, most of us have the inherent physical ability if we will discipline ourselves to reach the required level of physical fitness. If, after making some effort at this discipline, you decide to confine the physical part of your teaching abilities to arising from a soft bed, transporting yourself and your few ounces of teaching materials by means of a multi-horsepowered vehicle to a comfortable, dry, clean classroom at the church, you may be the loser! Why not make the best of both worlds? Determine to put into practice personally an element of personal growth which every good trail leader will want to encourage in the lives of campers for whom he or she is responsible. That element is stress. Stress is not only a necessary factor in physiological development, ''it is equally the basis of all growth: mental, emotional, and spiritual as well as physical.'' [10] It can be used creatively and constructively for personal growth as one responds to the demands of a wilderness situation.

Through stress experiences (and a *consistent* program of training for physical fitness can be just that!), self-discoveries are made that are basic to self-esteem. Self-confidence grows, and insights are gained into the qualities of personal well-being. Pushing yourself to a predetermined limit—and beyond—by exploring areas of accomplishment you once thought personally beyond reach will encourage you to take a new look at personal values. Wilderness leaders will achieve new spiritual vantage points when they push themselves to—and beyond—their preset notions of what their capabilities are, for it is at just such vantage points that God is discovered afresh. A new vista of God's activity means increased opportunities for exciting discoveries of life's vital lessons, along with the chance to enjoy the resulting satisfaction that comes with new growth.

Most manuals emphasize the importance of preconditioning hikes. This is good. I would also recommend a *year-round* program of walking, jogging, stair climbing—or a combination of these. It is not how *fast* you walk or run, or even how *far*; what is important is developing a muscle tone as well as conditioning the most important muscle in your body, your heart. Develop your own routine of exercise, and conscientiously work at it at least three times a week! You will feel better, think better, and should be able at least to keep the back side of your campers in view on your next trail outing. Some helpful ideas for physical conditioning will be found in Appendix F.

A word about the camper medical release slip.

A medical release slip is a must. Should a camper require hospital care, a permission slip, signed by a parent, allows that to take place as soon as the person needing help is brought to a hospital. The whole process of evacuating someone from a wilderness situation is beyond the scope of this manual, but the procedure is covered in the Mountaineering First Aid Manual listed in the Resource Bibliography. Remember, *no* understanding between parent and wilderness leaders, "written or otherwise, relieves leaders from legal responsibility for tragedy resulting from negligence." [11]

Chapter 5

Special Skills for Wilderness Learning

Whenever one enters into a new experience, it is natural to interpret that experience in terms of previous experiences. Much of our wilderness trail experience will have meaning because it relates to our existing frame of reference for knowledge. A person with a background in plant life spends hours identifying and enjoying the variety of vegetation in the wilderness. Another person with basic skills in camp craft finds pleasure in sharpening those skills under real life conditions. Building a fire, preparing a meal, pitching a tent—each of these activities becomes a satisfying work of art, more so if the minimum of accessories are available. The satisfaction of putting skills and information together is meaningful.

This pattern of learning is a familiar one, usually producing positive results. As our pool of knowledge increases, we are better able to meet new situations, decipher new mysteries, and appreciate the resources within and about us as we live life. Able teachers provide methodology. Information, presented with authority, contributes to our pool of knowledge and provides stability as well as direction for our learning.

All this is good, but does it meet satisfactorily the natural inclination to learn creatively? Do we believe the conflict between a person and his or her sense of identity will disappear just because mountains of accumulated data are presented? Do we spend enough time wrestling with the deepest questions of our minds to determine the who, what, and why of our existence? Can we move beyond pages of biblical information to a vital awareness of a confrontation with the living God in the depths of our being?

The church is endeavoring to deal creatively with these questions. Our responsibility in the ministry of trail camping is to make certain that we support and enhance the efforts being made in our church schools and site camps. We must capitalize on the environment as a natural enabler of the educational process. We do not go into the wilderness merely to test either our strength or our ability to survive. "Rather, the emphasis is on the qualities of awareness, identity, individuality, self-expression, contemplation, and harmony—becoming one with nature, flowing easily and living simply and honestly within the environment." [1]

When I write about special skills for wilderness education, the reference is to skills which may lend themselves in a unique way to ministry in a wilderness setting. They may not be new to the educational scene, but they certainly can be used in creative ways to open windows new to the campers. Basic camping skills are necessary to survival. Creative use of the special skills discussed in this chapter may lead to a new appreciation of life after survival.

VALUES-CLARIFICATION SKILLS

Life continually thrusts us into situations which call for our best thought. We form opinions which help us make decisions which lead to action. "Everything we do, every decision we make and course of action we take, is based on our consciously or unconsciously held beliefs, attitudes and values." [2] How does the teacher or trail leader guide youth in the process of adequately coming to grips with their beliefs, attitudes and values? In looking for answers an additional question comes to mind: "Is it possible to find in the wilderness an environment which will be conducive to a rational/feeling approach in answering the above question?" I believe the answer is yes.

Conditions on the trail force us to demonstrate how well we cope with situations under adverse circumstances. The veneer, or facade, behind which we hide becomes uncomfortably thin under some of the physical and sociological conditions on the trail. Realizing this fact may help one strive for more open and objective relationships in that sociological framework. This striving leads to a genuineness which is necessary in seeking helpful understanding of the supreme concerns of life in a rational/feeling way.

Guiding the decison-making process.

Leaders may take a number of approaches in trying to guide youth in making decisions. One approach is moralizing. An immediate problem with this approach is lack of consistency, sometimes in the life of the one who is setting the moral standard! Youth are also aware of the inconsistencies that may surface when young people are subjected to the moralizing of more than one person. The alternative, then, is to make up their own minds, a most difficult task when confronted with peer pressure or authoritarian adults. Powerful media pressure may already have left its influence.

A second approach is to allow the youth to do as they think best. The assumption is that if I intervene, I will be interfering with the one making the decision. I vividly remember a point a psychologist made as he discussed the dynamics of youth and freedom. Youth want their freedom, but they also want to know what the limits of that freedom are. Limits are to freedom what railings are to the Golden Gate Bridge! They keep us from making choices that are disastrous. Some of the longer, more dangerous log crossings over wilderness rivers have a safety wire stretched parallel to the crossing log. Some youth gladly cling to the wire as they cross; others appear to ignore it but close observation reveals their awareness of that safety line—just in case!

Still another approach is that of modeling. The danger here is similar to the dangers found in moralizing. Who is the best model to follow? Are people who model new standards to be avoided? Is the "tried and true" model always the best? How do youth establish their own sense of identity? The danger in each of the three approaches is the incon-sistency which we can often observe. The wilderness leader, working within the framework of the Christian faith has a basis for his or her morality in Jesus Christ—"Let your manner of life be worthy of the gospel of Christ" (Philippians 1:27). Freedom is interpreted within the biblical framework:

> For you were called to freedom, brethren; only do not use your freedom as an opportunity for the flesh, but through love be servants of one another (Galatians 5:13).

The leader who sets "the believers an example in speech and conduct, in love, in faith, in purity" (1 Timothy 4:12) will go far in establishing a high level of consistency in modeling his or her faith.

The values-clarification approach.

The preceding approaches will appear in varying degrees of intensity in our ministry to youth in wilderness education. We need to be cog-nizant of the ways in which our influence is made known. However, the values-clarification approach provides a helpful framework in which all persons involved in the educational experience can better understand the decision-making process.

> Values are the bases upon which persons decide what they are for and against, or where they are going and why. The lives of persons with clear values have direction and meaning.[3]

Values clarification is a special skill with good potential for wilderness education.

Basic to this approach is the awareness that "values and valuing are personal, often gradual accommodations to new ideas, attitudes, and beliefs."[4] They are not arrived at in a flash. Personal experience is the major contributing factor, with development and change taking place throughout our lifetimes. If we can enable campers to sharpen this process during their wilderness experience, we will have made a valuable contribution to their growth and development.

Seven subprocesses, grouped under three major processes, provide the pattern which evolves a personal set of values.

1. Choosing one's beliefs and behaviors.
   a) Choosing from alternatives.
   b) Choosing after consideration of consequences.
   c) Choosing freely.
2. Prizing one's beliefs and behaviors.
   a) Prizing and cherishing.
   b) Publicly affirming.
3. Acting on one's beliefs.
   a) Acting.
   b) Acting with a pattern, consistency and repetition.[5]

Part of the rationale for utilizing these processes lies in their becoming a natural part of the approach to decision making. The wilderness leader will want to help the camper become aware of beliefs and values which he or she prizes, beliefs and values for which he or she is willing to stand firm. The leader will use resources and methods designed to encourage alternative modes of thinking and acting. The leader will try to be aware of campers' actions in relationship to their stated beliefs and will seek to interpret what he or she sees in a helpful way. The ultimate meaning may best be understood by the campers as they find opportunity to "field test" the process.

Helpful insights in getting started.

The following suggestions, adapted from the article "Values Clarification: Some Thoughts on How to Get Started'' by Joel Goodman, offer helpful insights to the leader who wants to develop values-clarification skills:

1. Try to create a safe [learning] environment, one in which [campers and leaders] have a right to pass, one in which their statements are accepted. It is crucial that we respect each others' space and privacy. Try to avoid moralizing, and imposing or deposing others' values. Attempt to expose your values whenever appropriate.

2. Try to experience values clarification as much as possible yourself by reading and participating in . . . activities with the [campers]. Be willing to take the same kind of risks which you ask your [campers] to take. The more personal experience you have with values clarification, the easier it will be for you to [put your skills into practice].

3. Start by using values activities and clarifying responses. . . . Be flexible. There is no one recipe for being a values clarification facilitator.

4. Remember that values clarification can be fun, but that it is not for fun.

5. Diagnose the [campers'] needs and interests. Build your activities and lessons to speak to them. Later, call upon the [campers] to help generate new strategies.

6. Examine continually your role and values as a [leader]. This is crucial . . . in terms of your personal growth. . . .

7. Focus your curriculum on the development of skills in these areas:
   a) Cognitive—choosing freely (e.g., dealing with peer pressure), choosing from among alternatives, choosing with an awareness of the consequences of one's choices, being aware of patterns in one's life, thinking critically . . . , thinking divergently.
   b) Affective—identifying and acknowledging feelings as one data source in making decisions, legitimizing one's intuition as another possible data source, focusing on what one prizes and cherishes.
   c) Active—acting on one's choices . . . , goal setting, achievement motivation, culling out the inconsistencies between what one would like to do and what one is likely to do.
   d) Interpersonal—publicly affirming one's choices where appropriate, sending ''I'' messages, empathic listening, resolving conflict situations, asking clarifying questions, community building . . . , validating. . . . In this way, the activities and clarifying responses . . . will be given direction and purpose.

8. Start with lower risk activities. Provide opportunities for differing levels of risk. Alternate the arenas in which participation occurs, e.g., individual reflection, journal writing, small group sharing, and [total] group discussion. . . .

9. Encourage [campers to keep an ongoing daily log]. This can help them inventory their growth over time and become aware of the cumulative effects of the values clarification approach.

10. Solicit feedback and encourage feedforward from the campers. . . .
11. Try to wean yourself away from structured values clarification activities. Develop your own activities; move toward spontaneity. . . .
12. Be sensitive to the needs and readiness of the [campers]. Stay tuned to [them].[6]

Practical exercises in values clarification.

The development of our own activities for using skills in values clarification is important but difficult with limited prior experience. The following examples are basic exercises which may be adapted or modified for use in wilderness programs.

Values Grid.[7] Have sheets available with the grid and accompanying instructions printed as follows:

Issue	1	2	3	4	5	6	7
1.							
2.							
3.							
4.							
5.							

The horizontal numbers represent the following questions:
1. Are you *proud* of (do you prize or cherish) your position?
2. Have you *publicly affirmed* your position?
3. Have you chosen your position from *alternatives?*
4. Have you chosen your position after *thoughtful consideration* of the pros and cons and consequences?
5. Have you chosen your position *freely?*
6. Have you *acted* on or done anything about your beliefs?
7. Have you acted with *repetition,* pattern or consistency on this issue?

Beside the vertical numbers list the issues being considered. The campers may contribute these spontaneously, thus buying into the process. Suggestions might include pollution, cutting switchbacks, or cutting limbs from a living tree for a campfire. Campers will indicate individually their responses to the questions on each issue by checking the appropriate square. When all have completed the exercise, discuss the responses in dyads or triads. The purpose is not to defend their positions but to evaluate how they arrived at each one and how firm they are in their beliefs.

Rank-Order Questions.[8] These can be developed and printed on a sheet of paper. Once the pattern is established, campers may suggest questions dealing with issues with which they are concerned.

Which would you like to do most?

_____ hike

_____ ride horseback

_____ ride a tramway

Whom do you like least?

_____ horseback rider

_____ hiker with two big dogs

_____ hiker who drags feet in dust

If you were lost for twenty-four hours, which would you rather have with you?

_____ Bible

_____ *Decline and Fall of the Roman Empire*

_____ Western novel

A variation might be the either/or forced choice:

Are you

_____ more leader than follower?

_____ more physical or mental?

_____ more like a mountain or a valley?

_____ more like a river or a pond?

Have those with like responses team up and discuss their answers. Remember, the purpose is not to defend their positions but to evaluate how they arrived at each and how firm they are in their beliefs. After a few minutes have different respondents team up for discussion of their answers.

Values Continuum.[9] The purpose of this exercise is to have all campers identify where they see themselves with regard to an issue. Each will indicate where he or she is—close to an extreme or somewhere in between—and will discuss his or her position after all have participated. I give four examples illustrating the possibilities for this exercise. Campers will enjoy making up more. Each camper should check where he or she falls on the continuum.

Litter:
Pack it out   / / / / / /   Bury it
Trail food:
Eat-it-all-Paul   / / / / / /   Pick-and-leave-Steve
Campfire:
Biggest is best   / / / / / /   Small size is wise
Reflection time:
Very important   / / / / / /   A waste of time

Alternative Action Search.[10] The goal of this exercise is to try to bring the everyday actions of the campers more consistently into harmony with their feelings and beliefs. Vignettes such as I have suggested can be quickly made up out of true-to-life trail happenings.

Instructions have been given as to where dishes should be washed— not in a stream or lake but in water carried from the water source. Used water can be poured around the edge of the campfire or into the ground away from the stream or lake. As you wander along the stream, you observe a trail mate washing dishes in the stream. *Ideally, what would you do?*

Your trail group has broken camp, and everyone is ready to leave that campsite. Several persons have poured water on the campfire, but you notice that there is still a lot of dry ash in the fire pit. The group begins to leave. *Ideally, what would you do?*

Sharing.[11] This is a good get-acquainted exercise. It also heightens campers' awareness of communication/relationship skills. Pick a partner and share on a given topic (e.g., "Tell about the most interesting experience you had before you were seven") for three minutes. After three minutes find someone else and repeat the activity. After several exchanges ask the group the following questions:

1. Were you really listened to? Did your partner really hear you? Did you listen to him or her?
2. Did you really share your feelings or did you screen them before talking about them?
3. Did you worry that you talked too much? Too little?
4. Were you a "pickee" or a "picker"? Do you have a preference for which you would rather be?
5. Would you have added to your discussion if you had had more time?
6. Was your partner like you or quite different from you? Do you

like having a partner who is like you? Different from you?

7. Would you like your partner to have some of your experience? Would you like to have some of his or hers?

After an exercise is completed, or after a devotional discussion, you may wish to have the group share "I learned . . . " or "I realized . . . " statements. These may be shared verbally, or the campers may complete the statement in their log books.

The ideas shared in this section have introduced only briefly the many options waiting to be used to help campers discover what their real values are. The exercises are designed to make the individuals aware of their values through a greater understanding of their behavior, feelings, ideas, and choices. In identifying values and seeing them in perspective, each individual can come to a clearer understanding of his or her goals and direction for life.

PROBLEM-SOLVING SKILLS

Through a technique called "Initiative Games"[12] participants are challenged to develop problem-solving skills. This is done by involving them in specially designed activities where a problem is presented without the answer being given. As the group members face the problem they must determine how they are going to solve it. A plan of attack must be thought through. As they attempt to put their plan into action, they may meet with one, two, or more failures before they are successful. The activities are designed so that the solution comes about through each persons's active participation. They learn by doing.

The value of the initiative game process can be seen by looking over the activities suggested in this section. The camper's awareness of trust, responsibility, and self-image, which we seek to enhance through our ministry of wilderness trail camping, may be greatly encouraged by his or her participation in these activities. The self-awareness of the individual is strengthened as is group awareness. The activities used require group interaction and cooperation. Mental and physical abilities as well as the limitations of each participant must be taken into account. Becoming aware of the overall situation and responding to all the components of a situation are factors inherent in the problem-solving challenge of initiative games.

The purpose of initiative games.

The games focus on special skills including the campers' ability to become more aware of the factors involved in the decision-making process. Participants will also be given opportunity to become aware of their skills in learning leadership, and just as important, their capabilities as supportive followers. The ability to perceive individual and group responsibility in confronting a problem will be sharpened. An important added benefit is that participants really begin to get acquainted with each other. As the group learns to handle "game" situations, they will be better able to cope with problems encountered in real-life situations.

It is mandatory, after completing an activity, that the group "discuss and evaluate their participation in terms of leadership, followership, cooperation, precision, resourcefulness, flexibility, efficiency, and initiative." [13] The whole process of decision making should be evaluated specifically. Did someone naturally assume leadership responsibilities? Who was most vocal? Was the goal understood? Who was most helpful in shaping the plan of attack? What perceptions helped clarify the plan? Who initiated these? The identification and development of these skills will enable each individual to gain in the ability to cope with the challenges and problems of life.

The camp leader, in presenting initiative games, has a special responsibility to use them wisely. Be aware of the capabilities of the group. Problems presented should be solvable. There is no value in reinforcing failure. Be sure to take into account the age level of the campers as well as their physical abilities and condition. Safety factors and weather conditions are important, too. All instructions should be easily understood and complete. A clear statement of objectives and safety precautions is necessary before allowing campers to proceed on their own to resolve the problem. It is important to remember that group interaction has as much value as the successful completion of the task.

A sampling of initiative games.

Become familiar with the following activities and then use your own resourcefulness in developing similar games incorporating the guidelines as stated in the purpose of initiative games.

Game: Erecting a tent[14]

Problem: The group must erect a tent while all but one person are blindfolded. Without touching any other person or any of the equipment, the person who can see is responsible for getting the tent set up.

Location: Any open area.
Equipment: One tent.
                    Blindfolds.

Game: Lost!

Problem: One person, not blindfolded, leads the other members
                    of the group who are blindfolded about 100 yards away
                    from the campsite. Caution—blindfolded group must go
                    single file with a point of contact (holding hands, hand
                    on shoulder) between them. When blindfolds are re-
                    moved, the group must decide and verbally agree on the
                    best route back to camp *before* moving. The person who
                    led them to the spot does not participate.

Location: Wooded area
Equipment: Blindfolds

Game: Balance[15]

Problem: Draw a circle one foot in diameter. The entire group
                    must stand in that circle.

Location: Any flat cleared area.

Game: Feast or Famine

Problem: One of the group members inadvertently burned the di-
                    rections for the meal before starting to prepare it. The
                    group must decide the best method of preparing the meal.

Location: Campsite
Equipment: Cooking gear and ingredients for one meal. Put ingre-
                    dients in separate containers as packaged, but without
                    directions. It may be wise to have a spare meal packed
                    in case this turns into a disaster!

Game: The Monster[16]

Problem: Have the group join themselves together to form a mon-
                    ster that uses hands *and* feet to walk on the ground. It
                    must have one more foot than the number of group
                    members, and one less hand. Once assembled, the mon-
                    ster must move a distance of five feet and make a sound.

Location: Almost anywhere.

A reminder: Do not use these games as a "filler" or for a fun time
only. They can be fun, but they also have an educational purpose.
Follow-up is important. The value in initiative games is that they give
each participant the opportunity and responsibility to think through the

problem and determine or contribute to a solution. Talking over what happened provides reinforcement for successful individual and group participation.

AWARENESS SKILLS

I am very much aware of the stimulation that comes to our minds through the sense of hearing. This is so because of a radical hearing loss in my right ear. I remember sitting in an impressive chamber designed to eliminate as many environmental sounds as possible so that my natural hearing ability could be tested. In the stillness of that room I became aware of sounds I did not normally hear—sounds from within me!

Sounds, sights, smells, tastes, and tactile sensations are so much a part of everyday life that we scarcely are aware of them, unless something happens to diminish our capability to experience them. Even then we may never have learned to appreciate what has been lost. As we hiked a particularly scenic portion of a wilderness trail, one young lad was obviously bothered by the number of times we stopped to take in the view. Each step brought a new perspective to an already breathtaking panorama. It seemed nonsensical to concentrate on getting from point A to point B without stopping to use our eyes to appreciate what was in between. Finally he blurted out, "Why do we keep stopping? Once you've seen it—you've seen it!" I can only hope that by the time we reached our destination he had begun to have a new awareness of the majestic wonder of God's creation.

When we fail to cultivate maximum use of our senses we may discover that it is but a short step to believing that we can accommodate ourselves to the pressure-ridden and tension-strewn environment which we have created without any ill effects. But can we? The solitude of the wilderness and its opportunities for quiet relaxation fulfill a basic need for each of us. People need to take time to find a respite from the overwhelming activities, problems, and excitement that most days bring. We need this respite to get in touch with ourselves again, to take stock of ourselves, our thoughts and emotions. We need to get in touch with—and enjoy—the things around us which give us a fresh awareness of the pleasures of life. Cultivating the maximum use of our senses is an important way of doing this.

The value of awareness skills.

An important key to learning how to avoid the emotional upset caused by too fast a pace of life is the sharpening of awareness skills. Awareness skills are helpful in teaching us how to cope with pressures brought about by constant tension of our competitive way of life. These skills are learned by discipline, and discipline is necessary if "sharpening" is to occur. The discipline is rewarding as our senses tune in to the beneficent pleasures of the natural world. The psalmist was right when he wrote, "The heavens are telling the glory of God; and the firmament proclaims his handiwork" (Psalm 19:1).

Take time to sit down or to stand still. Allow your senses to be sharpened. Observe the patterns all about you. Notice that each pattern is but a part of something much greater. Become sensitized to the essence of each experience, noticing how the limits of your awareness expand as senses are sharpened. Practicing the following exercises will help sharpen each sense. The practical use of our senses will enable us to be in closer touch with God's natural world. Developing these skills may help us to be spiritually and interpersonally more sensitive.

Exercise One: Touching.
Pick up a natural object. With eyes closed concentrate on how it feels to the touch of your hands. Rub it along the inside of your arm. Touch it to your cheek. Try to discover something by touch that you did not notice visually when you picked it up. Reflect on how touching may be helpful or hurtful in human relationships. Does this introduce a spiritual lesson?

Exercise Two: Tasting.
Select an item of food from the trail menu. Take a small bite and chew slowly. Identify what you taste in general terms, then try to be more precise. Salty, sweet, bitter, and sour are the primary qualities we taste with myriads of blendings in between. Savor the full range of whatever you are tasting. Does tasting bring to mind a new awareness of the efforts of others to provide tasty meals for your enjoyment?

Exercise Three: Hearing.
Relax in a comfortable position. Breathe deeply. Close your eyes and concentrate on the sounds that are coming to your ears. Don't try to name them but, rather, experience them. Be aware of the effects that certain sounds may have on you. Is it possible that our spiritual sensitivities may be sharpened by learning to listen? In what ways?

Exercise Four: Smelling.
This can be exciting in the wilderness with its many unfamiliar smells. Breathe deeply. See if you can identify where the strongest smells come from. Crumble or crush things in your hands and then smell them.

Experiment by sniffing, then moistening and sniffing again. Sniff the bark of a tree. Does your campsite have an identifiable smell? Do certain smells elicit special memories? Are these positive or negative? Are people involved?

Exercise Five: Seeing.

Lie down on your back and look up through the trees. Try to get a total feeling from what you are experiencing. Roll on your side and enjoy a chipmunk world view. Roll face down and focus on what you see immediately before you. Stand up and let your eyes sweep over the landscape. Focus on one part of the scene. Describe it to yourself in detail. Reflect on the biblical statement, "and God saw everything that he had made, and behold, it was very good" (Genesis 1:31).

As you become more skilled in using the individual senses, begin to use them together consciously. Find a comfortable place to sit down, preferably where you can rest your back against something. Take a few deep breaths and relax, becoming completely motionless.

> Let the natural world sweep over you. Within fifteen minutes you should begin to feel as if you're being engulfed. The life of the community takes up where it left off. Squirrels may play around your feet, deer poke inquisitive heads into your clearing, birds alight on your shoes! . . . It is not possible to describe the unitive feeling of wholeness which sweeps over (you). Go out and experience it for yourself.[17]

Does the feeling of wholeness separate you from others—and God—or draw you closer?

Awareness skills and the group process.

Two additional activities which approach awareness a little differently are excellent exercises for building total group rapport. The first one can focus the group's attention on what it means to work together or to fight against one another.

> Group members stand in a small circle with arms tightly interlocked. With eyes closed, each thinks of a particular spot in the [area] and focuses all his [or her] energies and thoughts on that spot. Then each member tries to take the group to his [or her] spot. A struggle follows as each person attempts to move the group in his [or her] direction. After a few minutes of struggle, the group should sit down and reflect on the experience.[18]

The second exercise is a good one to use early in the trail camp experience as you try to encourage the building of a group identity. It serves as a meaningful illustration of what oneness can be like. Have the group

. . . move together in a tight circle until there is no space between persons. Group members will attempt to become one body by breathing together and sensing the movement and mood of others in the groups. This can best be done with eyes closed and by concentrating on the movements and breathing of other persons. How long did it take to get a sense of oneness with other persons? How do members feel now about the group? What does this experience say about the relationship of the team?[19]

Not everyone will be comfortable with these exercises. This is not a game plan but an approach which you are free to accept, adapt, or reject.

Summing it all up.

Within the Christian context of teaching we have a responsibility to encourage a sense of belonging. Utilizing special skills for wilderness learning enables us to help each camper have an awareness of being more than just an appendage to the group. Each one must be encouraged to have a vital experience of belonging and functioning as a working member of the body.

The biblical imagery expresses it beautifully. "For as in one body we have many members, and all the members do not have the same function, so we, though many, are one body in Christ, and individually members one of another" (Romans 12:4-5).

Values clarification, problem solving, and awareness skills are some ways in which the wilderness Christian education leader will try to encourage the body to come together as a working organism. All campers will not have the same gifts, but each one can be encouraged to fit in and become an active and producing part. The wilderness leader uses special skills to capitalize on the natural inclination of persons to learn creatively. The individual finds opportunity in creative experiences to broaden his or her sense of identity, perhaps in heretofore untried or untested ways. The alert learner may discover that spiritual awareness can be an exciting inward/outward journey with impressions that last a lifetime.

Chapter 6

The Wilderness Experience

The long awaited day of assembling at the trail head is almost at hand. Are we ready? I know of no time when the excitement builds faster than the last few days before the wilderness experience is to begin. The months of preparation will soon be put to the acid test. The methodical plodding through all the steps of preparation—if they have been carefully followed—will pay off. Let's review those steps:

1. At a minimum of six months prior to the camp, the Trail Leader has been selected by the person or committee responsible for trail camping in his or her area, and has been assigned a date for the camp he or she is to lead.

2. The Trail Leader has recruited qualified persons to serve as counselors, ideally several months before the experience is to begin. The age level of campers involved will determine the number of counselors recruited. I prefer one adult to three youth in junior high and one adult to four or five youth in senior high.

3. Training seminars in the area have been attended by all staff persons. Several additional planning sessions have been held to discuss the philosophy of wilderness trail camping; to clarify purposes for the camp in accord with the philosophy; and to design Christian education materials in accord with the philosophy and purpose of the camp. Even though leaders may opt to use materials from this manual, preparation is still necessary.

4. Trail selection has been made. Unless you are thoroughly familiar with an area, you have sought help in determining the locale of your wilderness experience. You have checked with persons who know the area and consulted the variety of descriptive trail books available (see the Resource Bibliography). If possible you have

walked the trail—at least portions of the beginning and end—so that you have some familiarity with it. You have found out, for example, whether there is a required two-hundred-foot setback for camping at a particular lake and whether it is feasible to include that lake as an overnight site. (Two hundred feet may have put you over—or up—a cliff!)

5. The overnight outing for training of counselors may well have taken place on a portion of the trail on which you will be hiking. The agenda for your hike should have been decided by that time. Will you be moving each day, traveling from a point of entry to a different point of exit? Will you be hiking in to establish a base camp with excursions from that point? Will there be one or two layover days (camping in the same spot for two nights)? Will you be making a loop, entering and exiting at the same trail head?

6. As campers have registered for the camp, letters have been sent to each one (a) welcoming them to the adventure, (b) informing them as to the specific locale of the wilderness camp, (c) giving specific instructions as to where the camp will assemble (site camp, trail head, other), (d) informing them of the basic rules of the trail, (e) listing the equipment and clothing for which they are responsible, and (f) noting any other instructions necessary, including instructions relative to ending the camp (see Appendix C).

7. Be sure that each camper's registration has included important health data, permission, and release slip. If you must register campers on the first day of the planned period, do it some place where money and papers which do not have to go along can be kept safely until the camp is completed. Be certain that you know if a camper has allergies, bee-sting reaction in particular (see Appendix D), or other health problems. It is imperative that each person attending a trail camp have evidence indicating a recent medical examination. Wilderness hiking is a strenuous activity.

8. When campers arrive, again depending on the age grouping, it may be necessary to inspect carefully the clothing and equipment which has been brought. Most important items to check are *boots, sleeping bags, backpacks,* and *tents.* With junior highs it is mandatory that everything be checked carefully *before* parents depart.

EQUIPPING THE TRAIL CAMPER
Hiking boots.

It is surprising how little campers and parents may understand about shoes. In geographical areas where a mountain storm with heavy rain is a possible summer occurence, trails might be exceptionally wet and muddy and anything less than a good, durable hiking boot will not be appropriate. Suede hiking shoes are pretty—on dry trails—but are something else when the trail is muddy and wet! Caution campers against bringing a boot that is too stiff; a full steel shank is good for climbing but very poor for long hiking.

Boots should be *well* broken in. Some outdoorsmen recommend pouring water in your new boots, letting them stand for a minute or two before emptying them out. Wearing the wet boots will cause them to conform more quickly to the shape of your feet. Your dry boots should be carefully treated to resist moisture. Check with the shoe dealer to find out which sealant is best for your style of boot. At night place boots on their sides (cold air settles in boots left upright) under cover. A heavy dew on a clear night is just as devastating as rain! For camp wear, take along a lightweight moccasin or sneaker.

Sleeping bags.

The most practical sleeping bag to carry into the wilderness is one filled with a material like Hollofil™II, *not down*. Again, the basic consideration is moisture. I suspect it may be warmer to sleep in a snowbank than in a wet down bag. A Hollofil™II bag, while somewhat heavier than down, can be completely soaked, but after the water has been wrung out of it, it is possible to crawl into it and get warm! Hikers who have been stranded in wet snow storms owe their lives to this fact. Remember, a wet down bag becomes useless. It is almost impossible to dry out in the wilderness. By the same token, do not permit a hiker to go into the wilderness with a cotton-batting bag, which also can become completely soaked.

When setting up camp, lay the bags out early to gain loft (material "fluffs up" and insulates better). In mountain regions where cool, night temperatures are encountered, I find it a good practice to place an Ensolite™or blue foam pad under the bag as insulation from the ground cold. If you want the luxury of comfort, a cheap plastic air mattress will usually last for a week's wilderness camp. In areas where it is cold at night, it is a good practice to eat a light snack before going to sleep. This helps keep the body metabolism going so that the individual will sleep warmer. Go to the bathroom before turning in—if you have to go, you will sleep colder! Pass this information along to the campers; you will get more sleep that way.

Backpacks.

There is no substitute for quality equipment. The backpack is another one of those ultra-important items which must be in good condition. Inspect all packs before departure to be certain that all welds or bolted joints are solid. Make sure each pack has a waist belt. This is important in carrying the weight of the load. An important portion of the weight is carried on the hips. It is also imperative to check the stitching of the bags and straps. A repair that is relatively easy to make in the city can be agonizingly complicated, if not impossible, in the wilderness. Make sure the pack frame fits and is properly adjusted to the wearer. Do this before the group leaves the trail head and periodically along the trail.

Some items, like sleeping bags, are strapped to the backpack frame. Make sure that the straps are securely fastened to the frame. Also be certain that the fasteners on the straps are in good working order and will remain fastened. I shall never forget the look on one camper's face just after we had struggled up a long, sloping, snow-covered rise. We were the last ones up, and just as we took the last steps to where the trail leveled off there was a "snap." We both turned just in time to watch his sleeping bag roll about one hundred yards back down the grade!

Tents.

Folks in some parts of the country will consider a tent an unnecessary item. As protection from heavy dew, a surprise rain, or even pesky mosquitoes and "no-see-ums," I consider a tent an absolute necessity. A properly ventilated tent will even provide some relief from the hot sun.

I do not permit "tube tents" in my camps. Made of plastic, they do not "breathe," are not easy to put up, and can be downright dangerous to life if the ends are closed in because the camper has gotten cold. Because of condensation, the water inside can be worse than the water outside. I learned the hard way about tube tents. A bloodcurdling scream awakened me the first night of a trail hike. Jumping up to find out what had happened, I found another camper already busy extricating a hapless camper from his tube tent! He had pitched it between two small trees and near a slight incline. In rolling over for a better sleeping position, he rolled the whole tent down the incline. Caught in a tangle of smothering plastic and strangling lines, he naturally cried out in terror!

I recommend a good quality backpacker's tent with a rainfly. Usually we find six good tents with rainflys in a group of twelve campers, permitting us to sleep two to a tent. A one-man tent or a three-man tent can solve the problem for a coeducational camp with unequal distribution of the sexes.

A word or two about clothing.

It is better to have layers of clothing than large bulky articles. Warmth comes from layering, trapping insulating pockets of air. It is also easier to peel off layers as the hiker begins to get too warm. Wool articles in the list are a must. Wool warms the wearer *even* when *wet*. Since much of the body heat is lost through the head, every camper should have a wool hat in his or her pack. For bright sunshiny days a wide-brim hat is a must. For the feet a pair of wool socks over a more lightweight sock will keep the feet warm, and the double layer will help prevent blisters. *NEVER* let anyone in the group go barefoot at any time. We depend upon our feet to get us in and out of the wilderness, and a stubbed toe or cut foot can be disastrous. If a stream must be waded, remove shoes and socks; replace shoes and wade across. Once across, remove shoes, put socks and shoes back on. The shoes will dry, and as indicated earlier, may even fit better than before!

ORIENTATION OF CAMPERS

When the campers arrive is an excellent time to get acquainted with the camper and his or her parents as well as to double-check equipment and clothing. Be sensitive to the camper's physical, emotional, mental, and spiritual needs. Parents provide some good clues to these needs, knowingly and unknowingly. Be aware of attitudes. The greater your sensitivity and awareness, the more significant your ministry to the young person can be.

I find this to be an excellent time to answer any questions that parents may have about the hike. They may be in greater need of reassurance than their offspring, especially if this is the first wilderness experience for the young hiker. Assignment of the youth to their small trail group (three to five persons) might be made while parents are present. Parents of junior high youth will appreciate meeting the counselor who will be working with their child for the week.

Procedure for orientation.

The time for orientation of the wilderness camp will depend on the agenda established once the group has assembled. If we are spending the first night at a site camp, I will use the time after the dinner hour to do this. An excellent movie (for use in a location with electricity) to get everyone thinking about preparedness for facing adverse weather on the trail is "By Nature's Rules."[1] This is a film dealing with hypothermia. More about that later. Orientation is the time to talk about trail rules in general, to share something of the leadership team's philosophy of trail camping, to introduce the devotional guide, and to encourage input from the youth as to their expectations for the wilderness camp experience. A group which meets at a trail head must still take time for this process.

Distribution of food and cooking equipment.

Food distribution, as well as assignment of who carries what—cooking utensils, stoves, fuel, and other accessories—must be made prior to the onset of hiking. Prepackaged trail meals (four servings to a package) are quite handy. We have prepared our own meals, which proved to be nutritious and enjoyable, but the work of purchasing and preparing the food was difficult and time consuming. Either way, I follow the same method of distribution.

A menu is prepared, listing each meal each day on a chart, including the package weight (see Appendix E). A copy of the chart is given to each small group. Food packages are assigned to individuals within the group, making certain that the distribution is in equitable weights and spread over the week so that the weight of the packs is reduced at a fairly even rate. In a four-person group, each individual will have meals in his or her pack for four out of the six days with the final light lunch up for grabs (The first dinner will be eaten, usually, before the group is on the trail. See Appendix E). The name of the person carrying the meal will be on the prepared chart so that the group leader need only call out that name to locate the package when the meal is to be prepared. Preparation is usually in the small groups with an occasional community meal for variety, if desired. Awareness of the weight each one is carrying helps in making a fair distribution of stoves, fuel, and remaining utensils.

The use of stoves.

It makes good ecological sense to carry a stove. Wood is becoming increasingly *un*available, and in some locations a wood fire is strictly forbidden. A backpack stove is lightweight, clean, and the amount of fuel needed to cook for one week for a group of four is not burdensome.

Our groups have used Svea stoves almost exclusively, and we have found that they will require about two-and-a-half pints of fuel per stove per week in conservative use. We have two stoves available for each small group. A community cocoa pot in the morning, for example, will conserve use of fuel.

Good safety practices in handling a stove must be emphasized emphatically! Minor burns can be treated adequately in the wilderness, but a person suffering a major burn is a long way from medical help. The best cure is prevention. *NEVER* fill a stove near one that is lit. *ALWAYS* recap the fuel container and remove it from the vicinity of the stove before proceeding to light the stove. *BE SURE* stoves have been checked over and are in first-class working order before you leave home. Only persons who have been checked out on correct operating procedures should be allowed to operate the stoves. Shut stoves off immediately when the cooking task is completed. Allow stoves to cool before putting them away.

WILDERNESS HEALTH, ECOLOGICAL AWARENESS, AND SURVIVAL
Wilderness sanitation.

Sanitation and personal hygiene are important subjects to discuss before the group starts their wilderness adventure. We discuss this frankly, even in coeducational groups, and everyone is appreciative. A wilderness toilet is a rarity, and when one is available it is usually situated so that the user is in full view of the trail! At our campsite we designate a toilet area which everyone will use. Persons using the area leave a hat or handkerchief on a designated bush or tree branch to signal that the area is "in use." Curses on the person who leaves the area without reclaiming his or her hat! Latrines should be located at least 150 feet from lakes and streams and at least fifty feet from camp. A hole six inches to eight inches deep is sufficient. Too deep a hole retards the natural composting process.

For some campers, personal hygiene is a well-established habit. For others, the need for constant reminders becomes quickly apparent. Dishes, clothing, and bodies should be washed *away from* the lake or stream. Dishwater, leftover cocoa or coffee, or wash water should be carefully disposed of and not splashed over the campsite's plant cover. If you have a campfire, waste liquids can be poured around the edge of the fire circle. This also serves to keep the fire from smoldering outside the fire pit. If you do not have a fire, pour waste liquids into a hole dug for that purpose. Restore this spot to its natural appearance when you leave the campsite. Make sure every camper washes his or her utensils clean, and scald all eating utensils and cookware in boiling water after every meal. Hands should be carefully washed, especially before food preparation. There is no excuse for illness due to uncleanness.

All types of debris and garbage should be burned if and when you have a campfire. Do not bury garbage. Unburned foil and other noncombustible debris should be *packed out*. If someone has been careless before you, try to pick up their trash and carry it out with yours. Save some of the plastic food bags for this purpose.

Housekeeping tasks.

The wilderness experience provides innumerable opportunities for youth to do familiar chores, and to discover new ones. Encourage them to be aware of all that goes into creating a successful and happy community experience in the wilderness. Initiative building will suffer if the leaders always do the cooking and the dishes! It is a pleasure to watch youth grow in the ability to set up camp, prepare the meal, do dishes, build and tend a campfire, break camp, and do other necessary chores, especially as they learn to find joy and satisfaction in doing these tasks. Challenge each group to see who can leave the *least* evidence that a site has been used by human beings. A really good camper will leave an unspoiled wilderness for the next person to enjoy.

Health and hiking.

There are also some practical suggestions that relate to the business of getting into motion—hiking. How fast should a person start out? How fast should he or she walk? How far is a good day's hike? There are many things that affect a hiker's rate of travel: poor trails, excess heat, rain, and high altitude, to name a few. Even downhill hiking, while seeming easy at first, can put a strain on infrequently stressed muscles and become very tiring. A beginner's pace, with loaded pack, may be from one to two miles per hour on fairly level trail. This can slow to one-half mile per hour or less on uphill grades, depending on steepness. In similar terrain an experienced hiker's speed may vary from three miles per hour to one and one-half miles per hour. One can push these speeds to a faster pace for a short period of time. I do not favor putting the slowest hiker in the lead. The leader needs to be an experienced hiker who is sensitive to the abilities of the others in the group and who will encourage the slower ones to do more than they *think* they can do! However, don't set a pace that will make the younger or inexperienced hiker hate trail camping forever.

I encourage a slow, steady pace in beginning the day, or after an extended rest or meal break. After fifteen to twenty minutes on the trail, have everyone stop. This is a good time to check pack adjustments, retie shoes, remove a layer of clothing if needed, and to make sure everyone is into it. Teach hikers to enjoy wilderness beauty. They cannot do this if they are busy all day long looking for the next place on the trail to put a foot down! Take time to stop periodically to enjoy the scenery. Again, familiarity with the trail, awareness of the plants and animals of the region as well as the topographic features—being sensitive to the expected and the unexpected—will provide maximum enrichment for the wilderness traveler.

Wilderness first aid, essentials of safety, and survival.

Persons who are willing to provide leadership for wilderness camps should also be willing to obtain an up-to-date first-aid certificate. Prevention is the best cure for wilderness accidents, but if they happen, leaders should know what to do. Accidents do not always happen in the "other group." They can happen on "easy" trails. I slipped on a wet ground bridge, a split log bridge across a swampy stretch of ground, just three miles from the trail head and broke my left wrist. I set it while it was numb from the shock; my wife made a splint out of a big piece of bark, a sling out of a dishtowel; and, when I finally got to an emergency hospital, all the doctor had to do was put a cast on it.

Know how to splint a broken bone. Know what to do for a burn—an improperly handled cook stove *can* flare up and explode. Know the pressure points for stopping bleeding in the event of a nasty cut or puncture wound. A severe puncture wound requires direct pressure. In the event of a bad fall, any number of injury possibilities may be present, including a broken neck. Know what to do! Dick Mitchell's *Mountaineering First Aid,* published by The Mountaineers in Seattle, is an excellent resource.[2]

The Mountaineers also list the ten essentials of safety for those going into the wilderness. These are "a map, compass, flashlight, extra food, extra clothing, sunglasses, pocketknife, matches in a waterproof container, candle or other material for starting a fire and first-aid kit."[3] If you are tempted to include an emergency blanket, a small package of tinfoil-like material, save your money! A better emergency wrapping is a large plastic garbage can liner. Step into it. Crouch down and pull it close around your neck. It will keep you dry and conserve body heat while you wait out a storm, or wait to be found if lost. The liner is also an excellent cover to pull over your pack at night to protect it from the dew or rain.

In the event that you, or a camper, should become separated from the group and you do not see anything that you positively recognize— you *are lost*. The first thing to remember is that your brain is your best survival tool. Sit down and think through your situation. Mentally retrace your steps until you can recall where you made your mistake. Unless you are sure that you have found the right trail, *stay* where you are until searchers find you. Protect yourself from the elements, build a fire—for warmth, if needed, as well as for smoke to attract attention— and wait.

Hypothermia: How to recognize and treat it.

One of the greatest dangers the outdoor person faces is hypothermia. Hypothermia occurs when body heat is lost faster than it can be replaced. It can happen in temperatures that are many degrees warmer than freezing when an exhausted body is exposed to wet and windy conditions. The first sign is shivering, the body's way of creating heat. Most people begin to move around, exercising to keep warm. However, this will drain energy reserves and weaken resistance. The only way to stop the energy loss is to lessen the degree of exposure and get warm and dry. This is crucial because once reserves are exhausted, the brain will lose its ability to make good judgments; the victim will become unable to speak clearly and perform ordinary tasks. Without treatment the affected person is heading for stupor, collapse, and death.

The first line of defense is to *avoid* exposure. Dress warmly, use your rain gear, protect yourself from the wind. Nibble on trail foods to keep your body's fuel supply ample. The second line of defense is to seek shelter even if you have to alter your plans for the day. Avoid exhaustion; you can slip into hypothermia in a matter of *minutes*. The third line of defense is to *watch* consciously for signs of hypothermia in yourself and others during unavoidable exposure: shivering, slurred speech, incoherency, fumbling, stumbling, drowsiness, and exhaustion.

If you detect these symptoms, *respond immediately*. The camper may deny what is happening, but believe the symptoms, not the camper. Get the victim out of the elements and into dry, warm clothes, or a sleeping bag. Give him or her something warm to drink (hot soup is good but even hot water is helpful). In severe cases, the victim may have to be placed in a double sleeping bag with one or two other persons who will share their body warmth. Skin to skin contact warms most effectively. In any event, take hypothermia seriously. It is the number one killer of outdoor recreationists.[4]

In regions where extreme heat can be a problem, be equally aware of the danger of hyperthermia, or heat illness. Overheating of the body can lead to heat exhaustion and, worse, heat stroke. Adequate intake of drinking water and the wearing of loose, light-colored clothing, along with restriction of activity, can help lower the incidence of heat reactions.

FOOD SELECTION AND PREPARATION

In most of our trail camps we use foods prepackaged for backpackers. The selection and purchasing of these foods is handled by a trail-camp committee. A good variety of meals is available, and usually the committee will ask for preferences. It is a good idea to have several "no cook" breakfasts if, for example, the wilderness group will be breaking camp on several mornings. This will speed up the process of getting on the trail.

If you have a camper with special dietary needs, find out before camp starts. We had a camper who managed to conceal the seriousness of his diet restriction until we were well into the wilderness camp. Once his needs became known, everyone cooperated in trying to provide him with the portions of the packaged meals which he could eat. This was a stopgap measure and insufficient to meet his daily requirements. He survived but lost considerable weight during the week. Awareness of dietary problems before the camp begins means that arrangements can usually be made to see that the camper's caloric needs will be met.

Always have campers read the directions before they start the preparation of a meal and then read a second time. It is awfully hard to read directions on a food container after it has been in the fire! Incidentally, I also have my campers mark their eating utensils with an electric pencil, for identification purposes, before they arrive for camp.

CAMPSITE SELECTION

When selecting a campsite in the wilderness area, do so with extreme care. In well-traveled areas, use only established campsites and existing fire-circles in order to protect the ground cover. Look the area over carefully and assist your campers in finding the "right" place; then select your own tent site. It is a good idea to look *up* before pitching one's tent. Is there possible danger from dead limbs or trees susceptible to sudden winds?

Even in geographical locations with copious amounts of rain, it is rarely necessary to dig a drainage ditch around a tent. Select the tent site carefully so that the natural pitch of the terrain and the placement of the tent make this activity unnecessary. Be aware of low lying areas which could be inundated suddenly by storm runoff or melting snow. Ditching tents, burying garbage, and clearing fire-circles can destroy in minutes the ground cover that has taken years to get established.

If the group travels cross-country and establishes a camp away from the more popular areas, it can use the area in such a way that there will be no evidence of anyone having been there. Cultivate this skill. It is good stewardship of God's country. Whether you travel trails or cross-country, topographical maps are extremely helpful if not absolutely necessary. Index maps, listing the available topographical maps, are available free by writing to the Geological Survey, Federal Center, Denver, CO 80225.

THE DAILY LOG, CAMPER REUNION, AND TRAIL ANNUAL
Keeping a daily log.

I encourage the wilderness travelers in my camps to keep a "daily log." Leaders and campers alike are urged to write each day, touching upon any and all facets of the day's experience. This might include anything from how they felt after the first day's hike to some new insight into a happening in the wilderness which has opened up a new spiritual meaning for living as a Christian. Campers are encouraged to respond to the "To Write About" sections of the devotional guide by writing in their log. These logs are turned in at the conclusion of the wilderness camp and provide the input for the trip "Annual," which in turn becomes the highlight of the reunion which takes place some months afterward. If the camper has written reflections or private thoughts which he or she does not wish to share, this request is respected. The evaluations which the youth give are extremely helpful in assessing the strengths and weaknesses of the wilderness camping experience.

The value of a trail reunion.

The trail camp reunion is a special event for the campers. They really look forward to it! It doesn't seem to make any difference what time of year the reunion is held. The nearness or remoteness of the reunion to the conclusion of the wilderness experience does not seem to affect the enthusiasm of the participants. I have held reunions in the fall, mid-winter, and spring. Regardless of the time of year participation has always been close to 100 percent. One girl traveled a six-hundred-mile round trip by bus, choosing to spend her birthday away from home just so she could be with her new wilderness camp friends!

This intense desire to be reunited with new friends testifies to the value of the wilderness camping experience. It also touches upon the purpose of the trail-camp reunion. Any investment in the life of an individual is enhanced through follow-up. The positive values—interpersonal as well as educational—are reinforced in the reunion experience. The "do you remember?" conversations are a great way to laugh about the funny things that happened and to recall the lessons that came about through actual experiences. I encourage campers to bring along any pictures they took. These, in addition to the pictures in the annual, graphically stimulate recall of the total experience in the wilderness.

The format which has proven most successful in our experience is to begin with a meal. Surprisingly enough, generous portions of "trail stew" (not dehydrated!) are enthusiastically received and have proven to be more practical and less costly than trying to provide a more elaborate meal. Parents and siblings of campers are invited and have quite obviously enjoyed the experience. Younger brothers and sisters have signed up for trail camp as they became eligible, largely because of the exposure to trail camping at the reunion.

A slide presentation really captivates the attention of campers and families alike. Participants in the wilderness experience seem to enjoy being a part of the main cast in the visual presentation. In order to produce a good visual report, careful attention to the taking of pictures must be a part of the overall plan for the trail camp. Try to capture on film something that speaks to each part of the camp, from the arrival of the youth to the final moments before returning home at the conclusion of the camp.

It is also possible, with careful planning, to take pictures which relate to the ideas inherent in the devotional guide for the week. I encouraged campers one year to take pictures which would illustrate some thought from the spiritual lessons we were considering. With a theme from the wilderness testing of Jesus or from portions of the Sermon on the Mount, imaginative and creative visual ideas can be recorded on film. One might take pictures, for example, of rugged crags as a back drop for reflecting on Jesus' being led to a very high mountain to be shown all the kingdoms of the world (Matthew 4:8). Photographs of the very fragile and beautiful wilderness flowers serve to illustrate Jesus' words, "Consider the lilies of the fields . . ." (Matthew 6:28).

I encourage a time of verbal sharing, usually around the tables, with campers speaking to those experiences that had the greatest impact upon their lives. A meaningful question to which they might respond is, "How has your life been affected by the week that you spent in the wilderness?" Several months after a trail camp I received a phone call from a grateful mother of one of the campers which I greatly appreciated. She shared how her daughter's life had taken a new direction as a result of the wilderness experience: "I don't know what you did, but my daughter has gotten excited about her faith and has voluntarily chosen to become active in church again." The mud, sweat, and pain of the trail suddenly became very worthwhile in the wake of such a testimonial!

Putting together a trail annual.

The trail annuals are really the highlight of the reunion. A good annual is a lot of work but well worth the effort. The pictures and the recap of the week's experiences, written by the campers, serve to bring it all back into focus. I find campers treasuring this memento of their week in the wilderness for years after the event has become history. Not only is it a continuing reminder of new friendships established, but the written comments entered at the time of the reunion by campers in each other's annuals serve to keep friendships alive.

I put together a trail annual on standard 8½-by-11-inch paper with a heavier weight paper for front and back covers. The completed booklet is assembled and then is bound by machine punching and inserting a plastic strip binder. If you can locate an office where the binding machinery is available, the cost is minimal. Copy for the annual is typed and then mimeographed or reproduced at a commercial copy mart.

Pictures which are to be included in the annual must be available as the final copy is being prepared so that the spacing of the text will allow for the pictures to be mounted after the copy has been run off. Have enough prints of each picture to be included made for this purpose. Printing from a mock-up including pictures is too expensive and precludes use of colored photos. If you or someone you know can develop and print the pictures, the savings in cost will be substantial.

The booklet begins with a title page giving the name of the camp (e.g., Suiattle River-Stehekin Trail Hike) and the devotional theme (e.g., The Wilderness—A Time for Testing). On the title page I include a picture of a scene highlighting some part of the wilderness adventure. Beneath the picture caption is a capsulized statement pointing to some lesson symbolized in the experience of the week. For example, beneath a picture of snow-covered, frozen-over Image Lake, I printed:

Image Lake

A jewellike setting which normally in August would permit breathtaking reflections of Glacier Peak. Perhaps for us it symbolized the fact that conditions sometimes obscure the long-range vision of beauty—forcing us to take notice of the beauty that is close at hand. Our week together permitted many such discoveries.

The next page I entitle "A Word from Your Trail Leader." Here I share briefly my impressions of the wilderness camp and make a comment or two about how I see the happenings of the week in relation to the overall spiritual goals of the camp. On page 3 a picture of the total group is mounted with names and a brief thought relating to the idea of renewing and/or establishing friendships. This is followed by pictures of each small group of counselor and campers within the larger trail camp group. I ask each camper to include a biographical statement in his or her log book, which is printed beneath the picture in which the camper appears. The statement might include place of birth, age, hobbies, sports enjoyed, family data, school attended, and other relevant information.

Next I insert a page entitled "Our Wilderness Wanderings." On this page is a map drawn to approximate scale which shows the route of the trail camp, the elevations at strategic points, and the places where the group established their campsites. Major points of interest are also indicated. I give the total mileage hiked, the low and high points in elevation, and the range of weight carried in the backpacks. You may wish to include on this page statements like "We went to enjoy the beauty of the wilderness . . . to be challenged by its ruggedness . . . to participate in its solitude. . . ." "We learned that the wilderness provides the hardships, challenges, new experiences, and encounters with the unknown which are essential for *growth*. We gained new insights into how Christian truth can be put into action through intense and extended living in the wilderness with other wilderness travelers."

The next section comprises the main body of the annual and is a compilation of daily activities and insights taken directly from the logs of the campers. The day by day report with appropriate pictures makes for interesting reading and remembering. If you have an artist in your group, his or her drawings can add much to the appeal of the annual. This section concludes with a one-page summary bringing together the high moments of the experience while not glossing over the moments of pain and struggle. If campers have been encouraged to write down their insights into the spiritual values of the camp, use these in preparing the summary.

In the final section of the annual I include a menu page, equipment list, and devotional guide. These serve as handy references for future camp experiences. The final page gives the camp roster complete with everyone's address. I try to keep the cost of the annual somewhat in line with the actual cost of materials, most often just charging for the actual cost of the pictures which are included.

Conclusion
Wilderness Experiential
Education: Affirmative Values

Outdoor living offers many learning opportunities to participants.

"Camping unmasks its participants." So states the writer in a volume entitled *Mass Leisure*. The writer portrays the wilderness experience as a struggle. This struggle has the positive effect of creating solidarity within the camping group "only so long as the struggle is with nature— so long as the enemy is without rather than within."[1] The truth of this is discovered by almost everyone who participates in a group experience in a remote area. Struggle is one of the unique elements in wilderness experiential education; it creatively draws people together.

There will be times when differences between participants surface, creating tension—the enemy within. When this is observed I am amazed at how quickly the unifying effect of the common struggle for survival brings about a positive resolution of the tension—not always, but often enough to affirm my belief in the unifying effect of the wilderness experience.

Similar learning may take place in church school and site camp situations, but rarely as quickly or intensely. I firmly believe that the communality of the wilderness struggle is what precipitated the following comments taken from the logs of campers and leaders: "There's only one day left with all of us together. I'm going to miss everybody"; "It will be nice to get home but also sad to leave all the people I've shared these last seven days with. So I regretfully end this log of the last seven days of my life"; "It's neat to see the way our kids have *all* practically welded together." Masks had been slipped aside. Persons had been given the opportunity to look deeply into the hidden recesses of one another's lives. As a result, all had experienced growth.

The reality of the experience is another of the affirming values of wilderness experiential education. The pretend, make-believe activities which may have value in other types of learning situations are not needed in the wilderness. Bedrock reality provides an excellent opportunity for the development of self-reliance and the corresponding opportunity to put into practice many of our democratic principles of living. Independency and interdependency as related to self, others, God, and the natural world can be discovered, applied, nurtured, and fulfilled.

Wilderness experiential education complements the educational ministry of the church.

To proclaim the wilderness experience as the panacea for the weaknesses encountered in the various forms of the church's education program would be foolhardy indeed. However, I do feel strongly that there is no environment

> . . . better equipped for learning than the one God gave us—the rich abundance of the natural world. The natural surroundings can serve as a symbol of group fellowship and *koinonia*. All persons are different, but there are vital expressions of dependence and interrelatedness. Natural beauty may be a symbol of the social beauty of the group and a vehicle for feelings of group morale and solidarity, which often develop rather quickly in outdoor settings.[2]

Whatever the form of ministry, we must remember that the Spirit of God is not under our control. We cannot program God's activity. No matter how hard we try, we are not in control. Our responsibility is to come to the task of ministry—in church school, site camp, and wilderness trail—with hearts and minds open wide to the movement of God's Spirit. We have a further responsibility to seek the most effective ways to implement the insights we receive through this openness to God's Spirit. Because God has not given us a spirit of timidity, powerlessness, or uncontrolled mediocrity (2 Timothy 1:7), we can take whatever risks are necessary to become involved effectively in God's ministry.

". . . The means of Christian education is best understood as the actions between and among faithful persons in an environment that supports the expansion of faith and equips persons for radical life in the world as followers of Jesus Christ."[3] The faithful implementation of the principles set forth in this manual may provide the leaders of our wilderness camps with a growing awareness of the privilege and significance of this form of ministry. Discoveries will be made and experiences enjoyed, affirming that the wilderness environment can enhance the expansion of faith. The trail experience may well add the special impact to Christian education which will provide a new generation of young people who are equipped effectively for radical life as followers of Jesus Christ in today's world.

I believe that youth who are given the opportunity of a Christian wilderness experience will be better able to face the future with confidence. As youth contemplate the beauty and the naturalness of God's world, their minds may be opened to further understanding of the mysteries of life. A new awareness of reverence and love for all creation may lead to an appreciative partnership with nature, others, and God, in turn leading to a rewarding fulfillment of personal existence.

Appendixes

Appendix A: Devotional Guides

Sample devotional guides are printed on the following pages. If you wish to make a 3½-by-8½-inch booklet, type the material in the following order on two 8½-by-14-inch mimeograph stencils or offset masters (properly spaced, of course, to allow for cutting, folding, and stapling). On the first stencil at the top will be "Wilderness Lessons" followed by Day 5, Day 2, and Day 3. On the second stencil Day 4 will be at the top followed by Day 1. The next space can be for a general information statement. The last space is for the cover design. After you print page 1, turn it over and *reverse* the direction of printing so that Day 4 appears upside-down on the reverse side of Day 3. One further suggestion: type the material with only half-inch margins. See the accompanying diagram of the layout. Suggestions for additional guides follow the first example.

SAMPLE COVER DESIGN

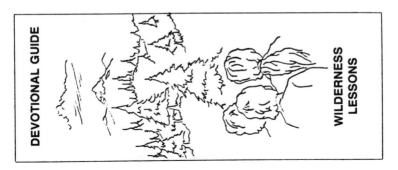

INSTRUCTIONS FOR REPRODUCING
DEVOTIONAL GUIDE

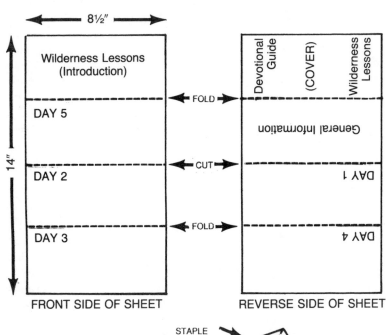

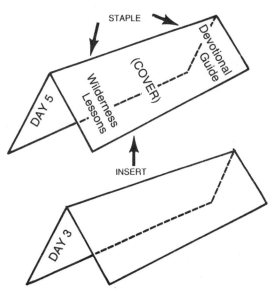

WILDERNESS LESSONS

Welcome to Wilderness Trail Camp! This little devotional guide has been prepared for your daily use. Some of the experiences we have each day will take on new meaning as we review them in the light of our Bible study. Some of the things we talk about in Bible study will take on new meaning as they come to life in our daily experiences. Have fun as you share together! It will be exciting to grow in Christ—individually, and as a group.

Read the Scripture for the day silently. Try to think of what it is saying in your own words. If you have a question about what it says, ask your counselor.

Be aware that at times we may seem to be going nowhere, or the way may seem too hard for us to continue. *But it's the small steps that make up the whole!* Our wilderness lessons will teach us that when we take one step at a time and press on, with God's help we will eventually reach our goal!

Day 1 . . . "New Adventures!"

Scripture: *"Thus says God . . . 'See, I am doing a new deed . . . I am making a road in the wilderness, paths in the wild. The wild beasts will honor Me . . . because I am putting water in the wilderness . . . to give My chosen people drink. The people I have formed for Myself will sing My praises'"* (Isaiah 43:16-21, *The Jerusalem Bible*).

To Think About: Do you get excited when you do something new? What are your feelings as you face a new path in the wild? Does God really take care of the wilderness? How will he take care of you this week? Is all water in the wilderness good?

To Write About: Try to express in your log your *real* feelings about this week. Share something you are excited about . . . and something about which you are apprehensive.

Day 2 . . . "Push On!"

Scripture: *"And let us not get tired of doing what is right, for after awhile we will reap a harvest of blessing if we don't get discouraged and give up"* (Galatians 6:9, *The Living Bible*).

To Think About: Sometimes the Christian life seems smooth and easy! Hardships and tough lessons are few and far between. At times like these, it is easy to push on, thanking God for our comfortable life. What kinds of rewards come when we "push on"?

To Write About: Record in your log your feelings when you faced a problem. Was it easy or difficult to keep going? Write down how you felt when the problem had been solved.

Day 3 . . . "God's Great Works!"

Scripture: *"Praise the LORD! I will give thanks to the LORD with my whole heart, in the company of the upright. . . . Great are the works of the LORD, studied by all who have pleasure in them. Full of honor and majesty is his work"* (Psalm 111:1-3).

To Think About: As you hike today, look around you. Watch for glimpses of the higher peaks. Don't overlook the little flowers along the trail. Do you experience pleasure in what you see? How does it make you feel? How do you feel about your trail mates?

To Write About: Pretend that you are writing to someone very special. Tell them, in a few words, about something that impressed you as being a "great work of the Lord."

Day 4 . . . "Lessons from Life"

Scripture: *"Look at the birds of the air: they neither sow nor reap nor gather into barns, and yet our heavenly Father feeds them. Are you not of more value than they? . . . Consider the lilies of the field, how they grow; they neither toil nor spin, yet . . . even Solomon in all his glory was not arrayed like one of these!"* (Matthew 6:26, 28).

To Think About: Listen for the sounds of bird and animal life. Do they have a different sound when you enter their habitat? What lessons can we learn from birds, animals, plants? Are we really more important to God than they? Why? Why not?

To Write About: List ways in which you think God takes care of you.

Day 5 . . . "We're Going to Make It!"

Scripture: *"[The righteous man's] heart is firm, trusting in the LORD. His heart is steady; he will not be afraid . . ."* (Psalm 112:7-8).

To Think About: Were there times this week when you were really tired? Have you gotten into any situations where you had to admit to a little fear? How did you manage? Are your trail mates helpful and considerate on the trail? Are *you?* Does the Christian have some special strength that helps him or her through the rough spots?

To Write About: List some things you learned about yourself this week. Did the wilderness teach you anything about God?

God Will Enable Each of Us To Reach the End of the Trail. God will not abandon us, but calls us to responsible use of the strengths or gifts God has given. For example, when it comes to crossing a creek, we may have to wade or jump from rock to rock. However, if that is not possible, we will use a sturdy bridge. When things are too rough for us, God will provide a way to get through the difficulty and to continue on.

When we are in an area where a campfire is permitted, we will have a campfire. We will talk over the happenings of the day and take a look at what's on the agenda for the next day. Each counselor's group will have an opportunity to lead in a short devotional time. If you have ideas for skits or singing, we will work those in, too!

THE WILDERNESS: A TIME FOR TESTING

Full of the Holy Spirit, Jesus returned from the Jordan, and for forty days was led by the Spirit up and down the wilderness and tempted by the devil.

All that time he had nothing to eat, and at the end of it he was famished. The devil said to him, "If you are the Son of God, tell this stone to become bread." Jesus answered, "Scripture says, 'Man cannot live on bread alone.'"

Next the devil led him up and showed him in a flash all the kingdoms of the world. "All this dominion will I give you," he said, "and the glory that goes with it; for it has been put in my hands and I can give it to anyone I choose. You have only to do homage to me and it shall all be yours." Jesus answered him, "Scripture says, 'You shall do homage to the Lord your God and worship him alone.'"

The devil took him to Jerusalem and set him on the parapet of the temple. "If you are the Son of God," he said, "throw yourself down; for Scripture says, 'He will give his angels orders to take care of you,' and again, 'They will support you in their arms for fear you should strike your foot against a stone.'" Jesus answered him, "It has been said, 'You are not to put the Lord your God to the test.'"

So having come to the end of all his temptations, the devil departed, biding his time. Then Jesus, armed with the power of the Spirit, returned to Galilee (Luke 4:1-14, NEB).

Day 1: "New Adventures".

Scripture: *"Full of the Holy Spirit, Jesus returned from the Jordan, and for forty days was led by the Spirit up and down the wilderness and tempted by the devil.''*

To Think About: Past experiences prepare us for new adventures. New experiences can be kind of scary. How do you think Jesus felt as he started into the wilderness? What are some of the good things that can happen in a wilderness experience? What are some of the dangers? What was the purpose of Jesus' testing?

To Write About: Try to express how you really feel about this week. Write down the kinds of things that you hope will happen to you (and to the total group). Try to think of ways in which the Holy Spirit might help you face the experience of the next seven days.

Day 2: "Food for Thought"

Scripture: *"All that time he had nothing to eat, and at the end of it he was famished. The devil said to him, 'If you are the Son of God, tell this stone to become bread.' Jesus answered, 'Scripture says, "Man cannot live on bread alone."'"*

To Think About: An old saying states: "An army moves on its stomach." As the week moves on, we will become more aware of the importance of nourishing meals, but is food our most important concern? What was the devil really trying to get Jesus to do?

To Write About: Try to identify the first temptation of Jesus with something that is going on in your life right now. How far are you willing to go to live "by the truth" as you now know it? Is the temptation to make a compromise always dangerous? If you can, write about different kinds of compromise situations that have come to you.

Day 3: "Winners Can Be Losers"

Scripture: *"Next the devil led him up and showed him in a flash all the kingdoms of the world. 'All this dominion will I give to you,' he said, 'and the glory that goes with it; for it has been put in my hand and I can give it to anyone I choose. You have only to do homage to me and it shall all be yours.' Jesus answered him, 'Scripture says, "You shall do homage to the Lord your God and worship him alone."'*

To Think About: Weather permitting, you have seen some of the most beautiful scenery in all God's creation. What is our responsibility to it? Think about ways in which our selfishness might destroy this for others. What was the temptation facing Jesus as he surveyed the kingdoms of the world?

To Write About: Write down one goal for your life that is really important to you now. Write about possible shortcuts that you might take in order to reach that goal. Tell how the shortcuts might hinder or help you in reaching the goal. Can God help you reach your goal? How?

Day 4: "Flying High"

Scripture: *"The devil took him to Jerusalem and set him on the parapet of the temple. 'If you are the Son of God,' he said, 'throw yourself down; for Scripture says, "He will give his angels orders to take care of you," and again, "they will support you in their arms for fear you should strike your foot against a stone."' Jesus answered him, 'It has been said, "You are not to put the Lord your God to the test."'"*

To Think About: Have you ever wondered who you are and how you might fit into God's overall plan? Do you think that one of the tests that Jesus faced was this question, "Am I really the Son of God?" If we are God's special people, should we have special privileges?

To Write About: Have you ever wished that God would show you some sign of which is the right decision? Write about your wish and why you had it. Describe what you believe about trusting God.

Day 5: "Time for a Breather"

Scripture: *"So having come to the end of all his temptation, the devil departed, biding his time."*

To Think About: Will we ever be free from temptations? What kinds of temptations have you experienced this week? How do you feel now about the wilderness? Is it a good or bad place? Has God become more real or less real to you? How? Why?

To Write About: Try to write down several lessons you have learned this week related specifically to ways in which this wilderness experience has tested you. How will these lessons help you live next week/month/year? How did Jesus meet temptation?

Day 6: "Back to the Grind"

Scripture: *"Then Jesus, armed with the power of the Spirit, returned to Galilee."*

To Think About: Good or bad, today's experience is a stepping-stone to tomorrow. Have you felt good about the challenges of this week? Do you wish that you could do some things over? Should we return to the wilderness now and then? Are times of solitude, reflection, and prayer necessary for our spiritual health?

To Write About: Describe what you think the Bible means when it says that Jesus returned to his work (Galilee) "armed with the power of the Holy Spirit." How is this power available to us? How will it be demonstrated? Jesus returned from the wilderness fully resolved to do God's will. What new resolves have you come to this week? Will your life in the days ahead be different? How? Why?

RETURN TO BASICS

". . . Don't worry about *things*—food, drink, money and clothes. For you already have life and a body—and they are far more important than what to eat and wear. Look at the birds! They don't worry about what to eat—they don't need to sow or reap or store up food—for your Heavenly Father feeds them. And you are far more valuable to him than they are. Will all your worries add a single moment to your life?

"And why worry about your clothes? Look at the field lilies! They don't worry about theirs. Yet King Solomon in all his glory was not clothed as beautifully as they. And if God cares so wonderfully for flowers that are here today and gone tomorrow, won't he more surely care for you, O men of little faith?

"So don't worry at all about having enough food and clothing. Why be like the heathen? For they take pride in all these things and are deeply concerned about them. But your Heavenly Father already knows perfectly well that you need them, and he will give them to you if you give him first place in your life and live as he wants you to.

"So don't be anxious about tomorrow. God will take care of you tomorrow too. Live one day at a time" (Matthew 6:25-34, *The Living Bible*).

Day 1: "How important are things?"

Matthew 6:25 *"Don't worry about things—food, drink, money and clothes. For you already have life and a body—and they are far more important than what to eat and wear."*

To Think About: Think about your values. What would life be like *without* your favorite food or drink? What outfit of clothes would you hate most to give up? What drinks are really important to your life?

Things To Do: List at least ten of your favorite foods, drinks, clothes. Underline those which are necessary to your life this week in the wilderness.

Day 2: "How much are you worth?"

Matthew 6:26 *"Look at the birds! They don't worry about what to eat— they don't need to sow or reap or store up food—for your Heavenly Father feeds them. And you are far more valuable to him than they are."*

To Think About: How do plants, animals, birds survive in the wilderness? Do we help or hinder their life cycle? What can I do to help? How does God take care of me? How can I help take care of myself in the wilderness?

Things To Do: Spend some quiet time, alone or in pairs, observing wild life (don't overlook the tiny bugs and plants!) Make notes about your discoveries. Complete these sentences: "The thing I like most about myself is ——————————————————— ." "I know God loves me because ——————————————— ."

Day 3: "Why worry?"

Matthew 6:27-30 *"Will all your worries add a single moment to your life? And why worry about your clothes? Look at the field lilies! They don't worry about theirs. Yet Solomon in all his glory was not clothed as beautifully as they. And if God cares so wonderfully for flowers that are here today and gone tomorrow, won't he more surely care for you, O men of little faith?"*

To Think About: Have you ever accomplished anything by worrying? What are some ways problems can be met, or even avoided (like tearing the seat out of your only pair of hiking pants)? Why are some living things very noticeable, and others not so noticeable?

Things To Do: Try to learn something about the life cycle of living things you see in the wilderness (plants, animals, birds, insects). Make notes in your log book. List some ways in which God has taken care of you during the last few days.

Day 4: "Does God really know my needs?"

Matthew 6:31-33 *"So don't worry at all about having enough food and clothing. Why be like the heathen? For they take pride in all these things and are deeply concerned about them. But your Heavenly Father already knows perfectly well that you need them, and he*

*will gladly give them to you if you give him first place in your life
and live as he wants you to."*

To Think About: Have my needs in the wilderness been different from
my needs at home? What is the difference between physical and
spiritual needs? What is the difference between "wants" and
"needs"? What does it mean to give God first place in my life?

Things To Do: Spend thirty minutes completely alone. Be sensitive to
what your senses are telling you about your surroundings (sight,
sound, touch, smell). Be sensitive to your spiritual needs. Can you
communicate with God? Do you want God to have first place in
your life? Record your thoughts and feelings in your log.

Day 5: "Live one day at a time!"

Matthew 6:34 *"So don't be anxious about tomorrow. God will take
care of your tomorrow too. Live one day at a time."*

To Think About: What were some of your anxieties about this wilderness
trail hike? Did they happen? Do you look at some things differently
since coming on this hike? How has God prepared you for tomorrow?

Things To Do: Reread your entries in your trail log. Can you write
down at least two things you were anxious about that didn't happen,
or that didn't happen in the way you thought they might? If this
week has given you new insights into the ways in which God has
cared for you, and if you have new feelings about your relationship
with God now, make a note of this in your log.

Appendix B: Equipment List

To Wear

_____Shirt (undershirt, if weather is cool)   _____Belt

_____Pants (should be loose fit-   _____Hat (one that can be
ting)   rolled or folded)

_____Socks (cotton inner—wool   _____Underwear
outer)

_____Hiking boots (*MUST* be
broken in)

_____In pockets or handy place: matches, knife, lip balm, handker-
chief, sunburn lotion, insect repellant, toilet tissue, sunglasses,
comb

To Carry—Try to Keep Under 15 pounds

_____Back pack (good condition)

_____Sleeping bag (Hollofil®II is best)

_____Waterproof stuff sack or cover for sleeping bag

_____Extra socks

_____Extra underwear—long thermals are a good idea

_____Extra shirt—wool would be good

_____Extra pants—shorts for warm days

_____Sweater or light, warm jacket (hooded sweatshirt), wool hat

_____Eating utensils (knife/fork/spoon kit and metal plate)

_____Sierra cup (metal drinking/eating cup)

_____Small flashlight

_____Soap, toothbrush, and tooth
paste or powder

> Mark your eating utensils and
> Sierra cup with an engraving tool.

_____Hand towel and small dish towel

_____Extra toilet tissue (important)

_____Any required medication (check with Trail Leader on this)

_____Matches (in waterproof container)

_____Tennis shoes for camp wear

_____Moleskin (for feet—blisters)

_____Tent (2 person with rainfly or plastic to cover)

_____Ground cloth (5' x 7' plastic)

_____Waterproof poncho or rain gear (*not* light plastic)

_____Ensolite pad (for insulation under sleeping bag)

Optional

___Camera and film

___Air mattress

___Water bottle/canteen

___Fishing equipment

___Compass

___Small mirror

___Knapsack for day hikes

N
O
T
E

Each camper will be expected to carry at least ten pounds of other essentials: food, stoves, cooking gear, stove fuel, etc., in addition to personal gear.

Trail Instructions

Hike single file; *always* keep person in front of (or behind) you in sight.

We leave *no* mess! All unburned or nonburnable trash is *packed out.*

We will work in teams of four—one counselor and three youth. Teams will prepare their own meals (food will be furnished).

There will be an equipment inspection and orientation on ____

_____ is the Trail Camp Director.

_____ are counselors.

No horseplay will be tolerated. We cannot afford any injuries or illnesses due to foolishness!

Appendix C: Sample Letters

July 24, 19___

Hi there, trail camper!

In just one short week you will be heading for one of the greatest adventures of your life—a week in our beautiful Washington Cascades, prepared for our enjoyment by God's wonderful creative hand. We're going to be learning firsthand just what God's exciting world is all about; and as we struggle up the trail together, scorch our stew, and sleep under the stars, we are going to be learning a little more about ourselves!

We ask that you plan to arrive at Cascade Meadows (approximately 13 miles east of Steven's Pass Summit on the White Pine Road) by 12:00 noon on Sunday, August 3. Bring a sack lunch for our noon meal together. The afternoon will be spent in orientation for our week's experience, including an inspection of your trail equipment to be sure that everyone has the necessary and proper items. We will have Sunday night dinner at Cascade Meadows, sleep in our tents overnight, and leave after breakfast for the trail head.

Several possible trails are still being investigated, and the final decision as to which trail we will use has not been made because of present snow conditions. We will not enter an area where risky conditions still exist because of either snow or high water.

I am excited about the adventure and the good Christian fellowship that awaits us on the trail. We have excellent counselors to lead us in our group experiences, and I'm looking forward to sharing in this adventure with you.

Sincerely,

Trail Camp Director

P.S. All good things must come to an end, and this camp will conclude after lunch back at Cascade Meadows on Saturday, August 9. If your parents plan to pick you up, 2:00 P.M. is the time.

February 19, 19___

Dear

Our trail camp reunion is set for Saturday, March 12. We will be meeting at our home at 3:00 P.M. Your family is invited to come along and share this event with you. Bring along for our viewing enjoyment any slides and pictures you may have taken. I will be showing a complete set of slides covering our week on the trail.

The annuals are ready for distribution, and I'm sure that you will enjoy what *you* have written as well as the pictures that are included. We will be talking about our experiences on the trail as well as plans for this year's trail camp. It will be fun to find out what your plans are for this summer.

Our reunion will conclude with dinner (no freeze-dried food!) and you should be on your way home by 7:00 P.M. You will need to bring $ ___ to help offset the cost of the annual. Let me know by return mail if you will be with us on the 12th. Be sure to include the number of people who will be coming with you.

Your trail friend,

P.S. Our home address is . . .

Appendix D: Special Concerns
The Danger of Insect Stings

Stings by insects of the Hymenoptera order—yellow jackets, bees, hornets, wasps—can be dangerous. About fifty deaths a year are officially recorded, but experts believe the real figure is far higher and that many who die of a severe allergic reaction to a sting are listed as heart attack victims.

Although it's estimated that 1 percent of the population is insect-allergic—about half of them severely so—most people are unaware of the seriousness of the problem and what can be done about it.

In stinging, insects of the Hymenoptera order inject venom under the skin. Normally, the venom produces a few minutes of fierce burning followed by reddening and itching at the site. Stinger and venom sac, if they remain in the wound, need to be scraped out. Simple remedies suffice—an ice pack, calamine or another soothing lotion, and antihistamine tablets to help relieve itching.

In a venom-sensitive person, however, the reaction to a sting is another matter—not local, but generalized or systemic. Even a mild systemic reaction—with generalized hives, itching, malaise, and anxiety—is to be taken seriously since it can indicate that the next sting may produce more serious, even life-threatening, consequences.

In the more serious reaction, there is anaphylactic shock, a combination of symptoms and signs that may include labored breathing, swallowing difficulty, chest constriction, abdominal pain, nausea, vomiting, confusion, weakness, blueness, rapid fall in blood pressure, collapse, incontinence and unconsciousness.

When a severe reaction occurs, immediate treatment is essential. In some cases of anaphylactic shock, death can follow within ten to fifteen minutes after a sting.

The key element in professional treatment is an under-the-skin injection of epinephrine (adrenalin), with vigorous massage of the injection site to speed up absorption. In some cases, a second injection may be needed in twenty minutes—and sometimes several repetitions. Antihistamine also may be administered and other measures may be required.

With such care the patient usually recovers quickly and may even be discharged within a few hours. However, professional emergency treatment is not always immediately available.

For this reason, many physicians now prescribe a lifesaving sting kit for sensitive patients to carry whenever they may be exposed to insects.

The kit contains a syringe preloaded with epinephrine, along with antihistamine tablets, sterilizing swabs, tourniquet and instructions.

One doctor states: "I strongly believe the public, especially sportsmen and those who participate in outdoor activities, should have on hand an insect sting kit and be knowledgeable in its use."

Avoiding Stings

1. Wear shoes and socks outdoors. Try not to seem like a flower to insects. Do not use scented soaps, lotions, shampoos, perfumes. Avoid floral prints, bright colors, and floppy clothing that can entangle and infuriate insects.

2. Don't swat a stinging insect. Move away slowly. If you can't retreat, lie face down, and cover head with arms.

3. Some physicians suggest taking vitamin B_1 (thiamine)—100 milligrams for an adult, fifty for a child—on a day you may be exposed to insects. It may help. The vitamin is excreted in perspiration, and the smell reportedly repels insects.

Lawrence Galton, "Insect Stings Can Kill." Full text is in "Parade" section of *The Seattle Post-Intelligencer*, 14 May 1978, pp. 21-23. Used by permission of Lawrence Galton.

Appendix E: Sample Menu

Sample Menu

(Meals divided among four campers—A, B, C, and D)

	Sunday	Monday	Tuesday	Wednesday	Thursday	Friday	Saturday
B R E A K F A S T	All meals are composed of prepacked dehydrated trail food.	Applesauce Buttermilk Pancakes Sweet Milk Cocoa A—27½ oz.	Orange Juice or Cocoa Eggs and Bacon Hash Browns D—20⅜ oz.	Cinnamon Apple Chips Natural Nuggets Trail Brunch Cocoa (no cook) C—24⅝ oz.	Cocoa Beef Roll Blueberry Pancakes B—25⅛ oz.	Cocoa Ham and Eggs Applesauce Hash Browns A—20⅜ oz.	Beef Jerky Trail Cookies Beef Roll Cocoa/Sun-rise Cereal (no cook) D—24⅝ oz.
L U N C H		Gorp Tuna Salad Mix Lemon-Lime Drink B—23⅛ oz.	Pilot Biscuits Jelly and Peanut Butter Spread "Ice Cream" Lemon-Lime Drink A—22½ oz.	Pineapple Chunks Chicken Salad Mix Pilot Biscuits Fruit Punch D—21⅛ oz.	Natural Nuggets Cinnamon Apple Chips Smoked Beef Roll Lemon-Lime Gatorade C—19 oz.	Fruit Bars Swiss Cheese with Bacon Melba Toast Grape Drink B—17⅝ oz.	Beef Jerky Trail Cookies Choc. Bars Fruit Bars 17⅝ oz.

	Sunday	Monday	Tuesday	Wednesday	Thursday	Friday	Saturday
D I N N E R	Tomato-Noodle Soup	Chicken-Noodle Soup	Tomato-Noodle Soup	Vegetable Soup	Peas	Corn	
	Vegetable Stew	Stroganoff	Vegetable Stew	Chicken-Rice Dinner	Potatoes and Meatballs	Chicken-a-la-King	
	Dumplings	Blueberry Cobbler	Dumplings	French-Apple Compote	Banana Cream Pudding	Butterscotch Pudding	
	Butterscotch Pudding	Lemon-Lime Drink	Orange Drink	Lemon-Lime Drink	Fruit Punch	Orange	
	Orange Drink						
	$33^5/_8$ oz.	C—$30^5/_8$ oz.	B—$33^5/_8$ oz.	A—$23^7/_8$ oz.	D—$22^7/_8$ oz.	C—$22^3/_8$ oz.	

Appendix F: Fitness Helps
Simple Exercises for Backpackers

Warm-up is important. Begin with stretching exercises:

Sit-ups   Knee(s) to chest   Touch toes   Calves stretch (push)

Here is an exercise you can do in your home. Step up on a box (or stair) and back down again. Start with one minute and increase as endurance builds. Resistance can be increased by adding backpack and also by increasing weight in pack.

For strengthening legs, especially for downhill hiking, hold weight at chest level in front of you and half-squat. Begin with light weight and increase as endurance builds. Do in sets of three with ten repetitions in each set.

Jogging stairs is good exercise. Build your endurance so that you can exercise continuously for at least twenty minutes. This can also be done with a backpack, adding resistance by increasing weight in pack.

Notes

Introduction: The Challenge of Outdoor Christian Education

[1] John H. Westerhoff III, *Will Our Children Have Faith?* (New York: The Seabury Press, Inc., 1976), pp. 24-25. Copyright © 1976 by The Seabury Press, Inc.

[2] Gordon E. Jackson, "Christian Education—A Process of Becoming" (An address delivered to the Professors' and Research Section, Division of Christian Education of the National Council of Churches, Omaha, Neb., February, 1958).

[3] Peter Blos, "The Child Analyst Looks at the Young Adolescent," in *Twelve to Sixteen: Early Adolescence,* ed. Jerome Kagan and Robert Coles (New York: W. W. Norton & Company, Inc., 1972), p. 69.

[4] John and Lela Hendrix, *Experiential Education: X = ED* (Nashville: Abingdon Press, 1975), p. 22. Copyright © 1975 by Abingdon Press. Used by permission.

[5] Westerhoff, *op. cit.,* p. 124.

[6] Carl Rogers, *Freedom to Learn* (Columbus, Ohio: Charles E. Merrill Publishing Company, 1969), p. 4.

[7] M. Alexander Gabrielsen and Charles Holtzer, *The Role of Outdoor Education* (New York: The Center for Applied Research in Education, Inc., 1965), p. 2.

Chapter 1: Wilderness Experiential Education: A Christian Perspective

[1] *Use and Care of Wilderness and Back Country Areas* (Vancouver, Wash.: Washington State Sportsmen's Council, n.d.), Information sheet.

[2] Gerard Piel, "Wilderness and the American Dream," in *Wilderness, America's Living Heritage,* ed. David Brower (San Francisco: Sierra Club, 1961), p. 27. Copyright © 1961. Reprinted by permission of Sierra Club Books.

[3] Paul Brooks, *The Pursuit of Wilderness* (Boston: Houghton Mifflin Company, 1971), p. 5.

[4] Garrett Hardin, "We Must Earn Again for Ourselves What We Have Inherited," in *Wilderness, the Edge of Knowledge,* ed. Maxine E. McClosky (San Francisco: Sierra Club, 1970), p. 263.

[5] *Ibid.,* p. 264.

[6] Phyllis Woodruff Sapp, *Creative Teaching in the Church School* (Nashville: Broadman Press, 1967), Foreword, p. vi.

[7] John and Lela Hendrix, *Experiential Education: X = ED* (Nashville: Abingdon Press, 1975), p. 163. Copyright © 1975 by Abingdon Press. Used by permission.

[8] Craig Partridge, *Who Needs the Wilderness?* (Article presented at the Wilderness Leadership School, Portland, Ore., 1974).

⁹William H. Freeberg and Loren E. Taylor, *Philosophy of Outdoor Education* (Minneapolis: Burgess Publishing Company, 1961), p. 192.

¹⁰Sigurd F. Olson, "The Spiritual Aspects of Wilderness," in *Wilderness, America's Living Heritage,* ed. David Brower (San Francisco: Sierra Club, 1961), p. 19. Copyright © 1961. Reprinted by permission of Sierra Club Books.

¹¹Freeberg and Taylor, *op. cit.,* p. 72.

¹²Olson, *op. cit.*

¹³Clarice M. Bowman, *Spiritual Values in Camping* (Chicago: Follett Publishing Company, 1954), pp. 39-40.

¹⁴Joshua L. Miner, "My Most Unforgettable Character," *Reader's Digest,* vol. 107, no. 644 (December, 1975), pp. 127-131.

¹⁵Richard A. Lovett, "Outward Bound: A Means of Implementing Guidance Objectives," Master's thesis, University of Toledo, 1971, pp. 16-17. Distributed by Outward Bound, Inc., 165 West Putnam Ave., Greenwich, CT 06830.

¹⁶*Church Camping for Junior Highs* (Philadelphia: The Westminster Press, 1960), p. 9.

¹⁷See Kenneth D. Blazier, ed., *The Teaching Church at Work* (Valley Forge: Judson Press, 1980), pp. 13-14.

¹⁸Freeberg and Taylor, *op. cit.,* pp. 113-114.

¹⁹John H. Westerhoff III, *Will Our Children Have Faith?* (New York: The Seabury Press, Inc., 1976), p. 23. Copyright © 1976 by The Seabury Press, Inc.

²⁰Randolph Crump Miller, "Theology and the Future of Religious Education," *Religious Education,* vol. 72, no. 1 (January-February, 1977), pp. 54-60.

²¹*Camp Administration Course Outline* (Martinsville, Ind.: American Camping Association, 1961), pp. 4-5.

²²Roy W. Fairchild, *The Waiting Game,* Youth Forum Series (Nashville: Thomas Nelson, Inc., 1971), p. 68.

²³*Some Thoughts on the Out-of-doors and the Christian Gospel* (no author, no date or publisher), pp. 8-9.

²⁴John Dewey, *Experience and Education* (New York: Macmillan, Inc., 1939), p. 13.

²⁵Bowman, *op. cit.,* p. 166.

Chapter 2: Understanding Adolescence: Guidelines for Involvement in Christian Education

¹Peter Blos, "The Child Analyst Looks at the Young Adolescent" in *Twelve to Sixteen: Early Adolescence,* ed. Jerome Kagan and Robert Coles (New York: W. W. Norton & Company, Inc., 1972), p. 64.

²Mollie S. Smart and Russell C. Smart, *Children: Development and Relationships* (New York: Macmillan Inc., 1967), p. 437.

³Group for Advancement of Psychiatry, *Normal Adolescence: Its Dynamics and Impact* (New York: Charles Scribner's Sons, 1968), p. 40. Copyright © 1968 Group for the Advancement of Psychiatry. Reprinted by permission of Charles Scribner's Sons.

⁴*Ibid.,* p. 21.

⁵Erik H. Erikson, *Identity: Youth and Crisis* (New York: W. W. Norton & Co., Inc., 1968), p. 128.

⁶Roy W. Fairchild, *The Waiting Game,* Youth Forum Series (New York: Thomas Nelson, Inc., 1971), p. 45.

⁷Smart and Smart, *op. cit.,* p. 438.

⁸Arnold Gesell, Frances L. Ilg, and Louise Bates Ames, *Youth: The Years from Ten to Sixteen* (New York: Harper & Row, Publishers, Inc., 1956), p. 138.

⁹Erikson, *op. cit.,* p. 129.

¹⁰Jerome Kagan, "A Conception of Early Adolescence," in *Twelve to Sixteen: Early*

Adolescence, ed. Jerome Kagan and Robert Coles (New York: W. W. Norton & Company, Inc., 1972), p. 94.

[11]Luella Cole and Irma N. Hall, *Psychology of Adolescence,* 6th ed. (New York: Holt, Rinehart, and Winston, 1964), p. 489.

Chapter 3: The Wilderness Ethos and Christian Education

[1]Joseph Wood Krutch, "Human Life in the Context of Nature," in *Wilderness, America's Living Heritage,* ed. David Brower (San Francisco: Sierra Club, 1961), p. 73. Copyright © 1961. Reprinted by permission of Sierra Club Books.

[2]John H. Westerhoff III, *Will Our Children Have Faith?* (New York: The Seabury Press, Inc., 1976), pp. 34-35. Copyright © by The Seabury Press, Inc.

[3]Ulrich Mauser, *Christ in the Wilderness* (Chatham: W. and J. MacKay and Co., Ltd., 1963), p. 14. Used by permission of S.C.M. Press, London, and Allenson-Breckinridge Books, Geneva, AL.

[4]Westerhoff, *op. cit.,* p. 78.

[5]Mauser, *op. cit.,* p. 29.

[6]*Ibid.,* p. 36.

[7]Ralph W. Sockman, "Exposition on 1 Kings," in *The Interpreter's Bible,* ed. George A. Buttrick, *et al.* (Nashville: Abingdon Press, 1954), vol. 3, p. 149.

[8]Alan Richardson, ed., *A Theological Word Book of the Bible* (New York: Macmillan Inc., Macmillan Paperbacks ed., 1962), p. 72.

[9]J. J. Von Allmen, *A Companion to the Bible* (New York: Oxford University Press, Inc., 1958), p. 283.

[10]Mauser, *op. cit.,* p. 94.

[11]*Ibid.,* p. 96.

[12]Oscar Fisher Blackwelder, "Exposition on Galatians," in *The Interpreter's Bible,* ed. George A. Buttrick, et al. (Nashville: Abingdon Press, 1953), vol. 10, pp. 459-460.

[13]Westerhoff, *op. cit.,* p. 75.

[14]Carl Rogers, *Freedom to Learn* (Columbus, Ohio: Charles E. Merrill Publishing Co., 1969), p. 4.

[15]*Ibid.*

[16]John and Lela Hendrix, *Experiential Education: X = ED* (Nashville: Abingdon Press, 1975), p. 164. Copyright © 1975 by Abingdon Press, Used by permission.

[17]John Dewey, *Experience and Education* (New York: The Macmillan Company, 1939), p. 115.

Chapter 4: The Wilderness Leader

[1]Richard R. Niebuhr, *Experiential Religion* (New York: Harper & Row, Publishers, Inc., 1972), p. 79.

[2]John and Lela Hendrix, *Experiential Education: X = ED* (Nashville: Abingdon Press, 1975), pp. 37-38. Copyright © 1975 by Abingdon Press. Used by permission.

[3]Victor Walsh and Gerald Golins, *Exploration of the Outward Bound Process* (1976), p. 16.

[4]*Ibid.,* p. 1.

[5]Hendrix, *op. cit.,* p. 36.

[6]John H. Westerhoff III, *Will Our Children Have Faith?* (New York: The Seabury Press, Inc., 1966), p. 6. Copyright © by The Seabury Press, Inc.

[7]*Ibid.,* p. 20.

[8]Hendrix, *op. cit.,* p. 28.

[9]*Church Camping for Junior Highs: A Manual for Planning and Administration for Junior High Camps* (Philadelphia: The Westminster Press, 1960), p. 49.

[10]Robert W. Davis, "Growth Through Stress," *Journal of the California Association for Health, Physical Education, and Recreation* (September/October 1968).

[11] Lloyd D. Mattson, *The Wilderness Way* (Chicago: Baptist General Conference, 1970), p. 8.

Chapter 5: Special Skills for Wilderness Learning

[1] Steve Van Matre, *Acclimatizing: A Personal and Reflective Approach to a Natural Relationship* (Martinsville, Ind.: American Camping Association, 1974), p. 208.

[2] Sidney B. Simon, Leland N. Howe, and Howard Kirschenbaum, *Values Clarification: A Handbook of Practical Strategies for Teachers and Students* (New York: Hart Publishing Company, Inc., 1972), p. 13. Copyright © 1972; copyright © 1978. Hart Publishing Company, Inc. Reprinted by permission of A&W Publishers, Inc.

[3] John H. Westerhoff III, "How Can We Teach Values?" in *Readings in Values Clarification*, ed. Howard Kirschenbaum and Sidney B. Simon (Minneapolis: Winston Press, 1973), p. 225.

[4] H. Ruchlis and B. Sharefkin, *Reality-Centered Learning* (Englewood Cliffs, N.J.: Citation Press, 1975), p. 145.

[5] Adapted from Louis Raths, Merrill Harmin, and Sidney B. Simon, *Values and Teaching* (Columbus, Ohio: Charles E. Merrill Publishing Company, 1966), pp. 28-30.

[6] Adapted from *Values Concepts and Techniques* (Washington, D.C.: National Education Association of the United States, 1976), pp. 145-147. For additional information on workshops, publications, and resources in values clarification, send a stamped, self-addressed envelope to Dr. Joel Goodman, Sagamore Institute, 110 Spring St., Saratoga Springs, NY 12866.

[7] Simon, Howe, and Kirschenbaum, *op. cit.*, p. 35.

[8] *Ibid.*, pp. 58-94.

[9] *Ibid.*, pp. 116-126.

[10] *Ibid.*, p. 198.

[11] *Ibid.*, p. 178.

[12] Benjy Simpson, ed., *Initiative Games* (Butler, Penna.: Encounter Four, Butler Community College, 1974). A helpful booklet presenting an overview of the initiative game process.

[13] *Ibid.*, p. 3.

[14] *Ibid.*, p. 58.

[15] *Ibid.*, p. 13.

[16] *Ibid.*, p. 40.

[17] Van Matre, *op. cit.*, p. 47.

[18] John and Lela Hendrix, *Experiential Education: X = ED* (Nashville: Abingdon Press, 1975), p. 47. Copyright © 1975 by Abingdon Press. Used by permission.

[19] *Ibid.*, pp. 47-48.

Chapter 6: The Wilderness Experience

[1] Available from Jim Lawless, Motion Picture Consultants, Inc., 1545 N. E. 130th, Seattle, WA 98125.

[2] Dick Mitchell, *Mountaineering First Aid* (Seattle, Wash.: The Mountaineers Books, 1972).

[3] Herb Belanger, "The Ten Essentials for Wilderness Safety," *Seattle Times Magazine* (May 30, 1976).

[4] Anthony J. Accessano, *The Outdoorsman's Emergency Manual* (South Hackensack, N.J.: Stoeger Publishing Company, 1976), pp. 14-15; and "Four Lines of Defense Against Hypothermia," pamphlet prepared by Mountain Rescue from the motion picture "By Nature's Rules."

Conclusion: Wilderness Experiential Education: Affirmative Values

[1] Gregory P. Stone and Marvin J. Taves, "Camping in the Wilderness," in *Mass*

Leisure, ed. Eric Larrabee and Rolf Meyersohn (New York: The Free Press, a division of Macmillan, Inc., 1958), p. 301.

[2] John and Lela Hendrix, *Experiential Education: X = ED* (Nashville: Abingdon Press, 1975), p. 72. Copyright © 1975 by Abingdon Press. Used by permission.

[3] John H. Westerhoff III, *Will Our Children Have Faith?* (New York: The Seabury Press, Inc., 1966), p. 50. Copyright © by The Seabury Press, Inc.

RESOURCE BIBLIOGRAPHY

Recommended Pre-camp Reading

Bowman, Clarice M., *Spiritual Values in Camping*. Chicago: Follett Publishing Company, 1954.

Brooks, Paul, *The Pursuit of Wilderness*. Boston: Houghton Mifflin Company, 1971.

Brower, David, ed., *The Sierra Club Wilderness Handbook*. New York: Random House, Inc., Ballantine Books, 1971.

Colorado Outward Bound School Instructor's Manual, 1977. Available from Colorado OUTWARD BOUND School, 945 Pennsylvania Street, Denver, CO 80203.

Frankl, Viktor E., *Man's Search for Meaning: An Introduction to Logotherapy*. New York: Washington Square Press, 1970.

Freeberg, William H., and Taylor, Loren E., *Philosophy of Outdoor Education*. Minneapolis: Burgess Publishing Company, 1961.

Hirshmann, Maria Anne, *Hansi: The Girl Who Loved the Swastika*. Wheaton, Ill.: Tyndale House Publishers, 1973.

Powell, John, *The Secret of Staying in Love*. Niles, Ill.: Argus Communications, 1974.

_____, *Why Am I Afraid to Love?* Niles, Ill.: Argus Communications, 1967.

Rohrs, H., and Tunstall-Behrens, H., *Kurt Hahn*. London: Routledge and Kegan Paul, Ltd., 1970.

Stewart, John, *Bridges Not Walls*. Reading, Mass.: Addison-Wesley Publishing Co., Inc., 1972.

Strommen, Merton P., *Five Cries of Youth*. New York: Harper & Row Publishers, Inc., 1974.

Todd, Floyd and Pauline, *Camping for Christian Youth*. New York:

Harper & Row, Publishers, Inc., 1963.

Walsh, Victor and Golins, Gerald, *Exploration of the Outward Bound Process,* 1976. Work manual available from Colorado OUTWARD BOUND School, 945 Pennsylvania Street, Denver, CO 80203.

Westerhoff, John H., III, *Will Our Children Have Faith?* New York: The Seabury Press, Inc., 1976.

Backpacking

Fletcher, Colin, *The Complete Walker: The Joys and Techniques of Hiking and Backpacking.* New York: Random House, Inc., Alfred A. Knopf, Inc., 1971.

Manning, Harvey, *Backpacking: One Step at a Time.* New York: Random House, Inc., 1973.

Merrill, W. K., *The Hiker's and Backpacker's Handbook.* New York: Arco Publishing, Inc., 1972.

Petzold, Paul, *The Wilderness Handbook.* New York: W. W. Norton & Co., Inc., 1974.

Environment Appreciation

Anderson, Bette Roda, *Weather in the West: From the Midcontinent to the Pacific.* Palo Alto, Calif.: American West Publishing Company, 1975.

Arno, Stephen, *Northwest Trees.* Seattle: The Mountaineers Books, 1977.

Kieran, John, *An Introduction to Wild Flowers.* Garden City, N.Y.: Hanover House, 1948.

Rand, Austin L., *Birds of North America.* New York: Doubleday & Co., Inc., n.d.

Van Matre, Steve, *Acclimatization.* Bradford Woods, Ind.: American Camping Association, 1972.

_____, *Acclimatizing.* Bradford Woods, Ind.: American Camping Association, 1974.

Developing the Wilderness Education Program

The Church's Educational Ministry: A Curriculum Plan. St. Louis: The Bethany Press, 1966.

Gabrielsen, M. Alexander, *The Role of Outdoor Education.* New York: Center for Applied Research in Education, 1965.

Hammerman, Donald R., *Teaching in the Outdoors.* Minneapolis: Burgess Publication Company, 1964.

Hendrix, John and Lela, *Experiential Education: X = ED.* Nashville:

Abingdon Press, 1975.

Miller, Donald E., Snyder, Graydon F., and Neff, Robert W., *Using Biblical Simulations*. Valley Forge: Judson Press, 1973.

Nelson, C. Ellis, *Where Faith Begins*. Atlanta: John Knox Press, 1971.

Simon, Sidney B., Howe, Leland W., and Kirschenbaum, Howard, *Values Clarification: A Handbook of Practical Strategies for Teachers and Students*. New York: Hart Publishing Company, Inc., 1972.

Simpson, Benjy, *Initiative Games*. Butler, Pa.: Butler Community College, 1974.

Thornton, David, *Faith Recycling: A Process for Understanding Your Personal Beliefs*. Valley Forge: Department of Ministry with Youth, Board of Educational Ministries of the American Baptist Churches in the U.S.A., 1974.

Westerhoff, John H., III, *A Colloquy on Christian Education*. Philadelphia: United Church Press, 1972.

Survival, First Aid

Accessano, Anthony J., *The Outdoorsman's Emergency Manual*. South Hackensack, N.J.: Stoeger Publishing Company, 1976.

Angier, Bradford, *Survival With Style*. New York: Random House, Inc., Vintage Books, 1974.

Brown, Robert E., *Hip Pocket Survival Handbook*. Bellevue, Wash.: American Outdoor Safety League, 1979.

Graves, Richard H., *Bushcraft: A Serious Guide to Survival and Camping*. New York: Schocken Books, 1972.

Kodet, B., *Being Your Own Wilderness Doctor: The Outdoorsman's Emergency Manual*. Harrisburg, Pa.: Stackpole Books, 1968.

Mitchell, Dick, *Mountaineering First Aid*. Seattle: The Mountaineers Books, 1972.

Wilderson, James A., ed., *Medicine for Mountaineering*. Seattle: The Mountaineers Books, 1975.

Regional Guides to Wilderness Trails

Bach, Orville E., Jr., *Hiking the Yellowstone Backcountry*. San Francisco: Sierra Club Books, 1973.

Linkhart, Luther, *Sawtooth National Recreation Area*. Berkeley: Wilderness Press, 1981.

Lowe, Don and Roberta, *80 Northern Colorado Hiking Trails*. Beaverton, Ore.: The Touchstone Press, 1973.

Macaree, Mary and David, *103 Hikes in Southwestern British Columbia*. 2nd ed. Seattle: The Mountaineers Books, 1980.

Manning, Harvey, and Spring, Ira, *50 Hikes in Mt. Rainier National Park*. Seattle: The Mountaineers Books, 1969.

——————, *101 Hikes in the North Cascades*. Seattle: The Mountaineers Books, 1970.

——————, *102 Hikes in the Alpine Lakes, South Cascades and Olympics*. Seattle: The Mountaineers Books, 1971.

Mazel, David, *Arizona Trails*. Berkeley: Wilderness Press, 1981.

Meves, Eric, *Guide to Backpacking in the U.S.: Where to Go and How to Get There*. New York: Macmillan, Inc., 1979.

Mitchell, Ron, *50 Eastern Idaho Hiking Trails*. Boulder, Colo.: Pruett Publishing Co., 1979.

Nienhueser, Helen, and Simmerman, Nancy, *55 Ways to Wilderness in South-central Alaska*. 2nd ed. Seattle: The Mountaineers Books, 1981.

Perry, John, and Perry, June Greverus, *The Random House Guide to Natural Areas of the Eastern United States*. New York: Random House, Inc., 1980.

Piggott, Margaret, *Discover Southeast Alaska*. Seattle: The Mountaineers Books, 1974.

Sullivan, Jerry, and Daniel, Glenda, *Hiking Trails in the Midwest*. Chicago: Contemporary Books, Inc., 1980.

Winnett, Thomas, *Sierra North, 100 Backcountry Trips*. 3rd ed. Berkeley: Wilderness Press, 1976.

Winnett, Thomas, and Winnett, Jason, *Sierra South, 100 Backcountry Trips*. 3rd ed. Berkeley: Wilderness Press, 1980.

Index

Adolescence
  chronological age, 43
  early, 43, 51-53
  late, 43, 54
  proper, 43, 51
Adolescents
  calorie needs, 46
  chronological age, 43
  creative abilities, 50-51
  dynamics of rapid growth, 46-47
  expectations of, 44-45
  independent thinking, 50-51
  physical characteristics and
    needs, 45-47
  psychological characteristics
    and needs, 49-51
  rapid growth, 51
  religious characteristics and
    needs, 51-53
  revolt against religion, 54
  self-acceptance, 49-50
  self-esteem, 49-50
  self-image, 47-49
  social characteristics and
    needs, 47-49
  solo experience, 50, 61
  television, impact of, 37
  value system, 54
  youth culture, 48
Advance planning, 30
Awareness skills, 102-105
Bible, the
  as textbook, 39, 59
  background passages, wilderness
    lessons, 60-68
  1 Corinthians, 68

Deuteronomy, 60, 62
Exodus, 60, 61, 62, 66
Ezekiel, 60
Galatians, 67, 68
Hosea, 66
Jeremiah, 60
John, 65
1 Kings, 62, 63
Luke, 65
Mark, 66
Philippians, 66
Psalms, 64
Romans, 68
1 Samuel, 64
2 Samuel, 64
Israel, 60-61, 68, 71
personalities
  David, 64
  Elijah, 20, 62-63, 67
  Jesus Christ, 31, 35, 53, 65-67
  John the Baptist, 64-65
  Moses, 37, 61-62, 67
  Paul, 67-68
questions for Bible study, 58-59
Campers
  awareness skills, 102-105
  calorie needs, 46
  coeducational camps, 29-30, 49, 81,
    111
  daily log, 39, 118, 121-122
  devotional guide, 87, 127-136
  environmental appreciation, 34, 86
  equipment list, 137-138
  getting acquainted, 98-99,
    104-105, 111
  hiking pace, 114-115

initiative building, 114
initiative games, 99-102
leader-camper ratio, 39, 107, 138
letters to, 108, 139, 140
limits of endurance, 46-47
medical release slip, 89, 108
orientation, 111-112
personal hygiene, 113-114
problem solving skills, 99-102
registration of, 108
reunion, 118-120, 140
self-appreciation, 86
self-awareness, 83-84
self-confidence, 84-85
solo experience, 50, 61
spiritual self-identity, 85-86
struggle, value of, 40
trail annual, 118, 120-122
Christian education
  goal of, 10-11
  statement of objective, 30
Church schools, 9-10, 23, 31, 83
Coeducational camps, 29-30, 49, 81,
  111
Community of faith, 11, 14, 59
Curriculum development, 38-40
Curriculum techniques, 35-38
Daily log, 39, 118, 121-122
David, 64
Decision making, 92-94
Devotional guide, 87, 127-136
Dewey, John, 27
Early camping, 26
Ecological awareness, 28, 34, 39, 85,
  86
Elijah, 20, 62-63, 67
Endurance, 46-47
Environment and learning, 70
Equipment
  back packs, 110
  camp stoves, 112-113
  clothing, 111
  hiking boots, 108-109
  inspection, 108, 111
  sleeping bags, 109
  stove safety, 113
  tents, 110-111
Experiential education
  environment and learning, 70-71
  ingredients of growth, 20
  learning by doing, 28-29
  positive effects, 69-71
  reflection, 28

  teachable moments, 23-24
  weaknesses, 71-72
First Aid
  certificate, 115
  insect stings, 141-142
  in the wilderness, 115-116
  medical release slip, 89, 108
  resource books, 155
  stove safety, 113
Food
  adolescent calorie needs, 46
  diet restrictions, 117
  distribution of, 81, 112
  menu, 112, 143-144
  selection and preparation, 117
  stove safety, 113
Forest Service information, 87
Goodman, Joel, 95
Hahn, Kurt, 28-29
Hendrix, John and Lela, 79
Hendrix process, 80-83
Hinkley, George W., 26
Holt, Louis, 28-29
Hyperthermia, 117
Hypothermia, 24, 116-117
Initiative Games, 99-102
Israel, 60-61, 68, 71
Jesus Christ, 31, 35, 53, 65-67
John the Baptist, 64-65
Leaders
  awareness skills, 102-105
  celebration, 82
  commitment to Christ, 75
  debriefing, 82
  decision making, 92-94
  devotional guide, 87, 127-136
  evaluation, 82
  forest service information, 87
  group building, 104-105
  hiking pace, 114-115
  inner resources, 41
  leader-camper ratio, 39, 107, 138
  medical release slip, 89, 108
  overnight outing, 77, 79, 87, 108
  physical fitness, 88, 145
  quality of, 75
  scapegoating, 77
  selection and training of, 86-89
  self-awareness, 83-84
  self-confidence, 88
  self-esteem, 88
  stress, 88
  team building, 81-82

Leader-camper ratio, 39, 107, 138
Limits of endurance, 46-47
Medical release slip, 89, 108
McLuhan, Marshall, 69
Murray, H. H., 26
Objective of Christian education, 30
Objectives of wilderness Christian
    education, 31
Olson, Sigurd, 26-27
Outward Bound, 28-29, 77-79
Outward Bound leadership model, 78,
    83
Overnight outing for leaders, 77,
    79, 87, 108
Paul, 67-68
Personality development, 34-35
Personal commitment to Christ, 85-86
Philosophy of learning-premises, 29
Rogers, Carl, 14
Role playing, 11
Secular camping
    objectives, 34-35
    art of outdoor living, 34
    constructive use of leisure, 34
    democratic living, 35
    personality development, 34-35
Site camps, 22, 25, 123, 124
Small groups, 13, 43, 79, 81, 104-105
Solitude, 50, 61
Spiritual self-identity, 85-86
Stewardship, 34
Stress, 29, 88
Struggle, value of, 40
Survival
    hyperthermia, 117
    hypothermia, 24, 116-117
    if lost, 116
    resource books, 155
    survival aids, 115-116
    teamwork, 22
Teamwork, 22, 81-82
Time schedule, 23, 107
Thoreau, 21
Trail annual, 118, 120-122
Trail camp reunion, 118-120
Wilderness
    Act of 1964, 20
    as experience, 21-22
    as freedom, 23
    as involvement, 22-23
    as learning environment, 24-25
    as refuge, 31
    camp size, 49, 87

    defined, 20-21
    regulations, 87
    spiritual values of, 57-60
Wilderness camping
    campsite selection, 117-118
    care of environment, 28, 34, 39, 85
    coeducational, 29-30, 49, 81, 111
    forest service information, 87
    hiking pace, 114-115
    integrity of, 28
    permits, 87
    philosophy of, 25-30
    preparing for, 107-108
    sanitation, 113-114
    size limitations, 49, 87
    struggle, value of, 40
    teachable moments, 23-24, 36, 40,
        70-71
    topographical maps, 118
    trail selection, 107
    training seminars, 107
Wilderness Christian education
    coeducational, 29-30, 49
    curriculum development, 38-40
    curriculum techniques, 35-38
        creativity, 38
        cooperation, 36-37
        informality, 37-38
        investigation, 36
        meditation, 37
        observation, 35-36
        participation, 38
    experiential learning, 40-41, 70
    genius of, 69
    goals, 32-34
        attitudes, 32-33
        content, 33
        ethics, 33-34
        relationships, 33
    objectives, 31
    philosophy of, 27-30
    spiritual self-identity, 85-86
    teachable moments, 23-24, 36, 40,
        70-71
    weaknesses of, 71-72
Values clarification
    alternative action search, 98
    decision making, 92-94
    rank order questions, 97
    skills, 92-99
    values continuum, 97-98
    values grid, 96